First World War
and Army of Occupation
War Diary
France, Belgium and Germany

42 DIVISION
127 Infantry Brigade,
Brigade Machine Gun Company
1 March 1917 - 28 February 1918

WO95/2661/3

The Naval & Military Press Ltd
www.nmarchive.com
Published in association with The National Archives

Published by

The Naval & Military Press Ltd

Unit 10 Ridgewood Industrial Park,

Uckfield, East Sussex,

TN22 5QE England

Tel: +44 (0) 1825 749494

www.naval-military-press.com

www.nmarchive.com

This diary has been reprinted in facsimile from the original. Any imperfections are inevitably reproduced and the quality may fall short of modern type and cartographic standards.

© **Crown Copyright**
Images reproduced by permission of The National Archives, London, England, 2015.

Contents

Document type	Place/Title	Date From	Date To
Heading	WO95/2661/3 127 Inf Bde MGC Ma17-Feb' 18		
Heading	42nd Division 127th Infy Bde 127th Machine Gun Coy. Mar 1917-Feb 1918		
Heading	War Diary 127 Machine Gun Company Period 1st March 1917 To 31st March 1917 vol III		
War Diary	Alexandria	01/03/1917	02/03/1917
War Diary	H.M.T. Corsican	03/03/1917	08/03/1917
War Diary	Marseilles	09/03/1917	11/03/1917
War Diary	Vaux	12/03/1917	28/03/1917
War Diary	Fontaine Sur Somme	29/03/1917	29/03/1917
War Diary	Chuignes	30/03/1917	31/03/1917
Heading	127th Machine Gun Company War Diary Period 1st April 1917 To 30th April 1917 Vol IV		
War Diary	Chuignes	01/04/1917	09/04/1917
War Diary	Dompierre	10/04/1917	18/04/1917
War Diary	Peronne	19/04/1917	30/04/1917
Heading	War Diary Of 127th Machine Gun Company Period 1st May 1917 To 31st May 1917 Volume V		
War Diary	Peizieres	01/05/1917	10/05/1917
War Diary	Longavesnes	10/05/1917	17/05/1917
War Diary	Neuville	18/05/1917	19/05/1917
War Diary	Ruyaulcourt	20/05/1917	31/05/1917
Diagram etc	Brown Line Left Sector		
Map	Appendix II Proposed Machine & Lewis Gun Positions Left Sector		
Map	Appendix III Position of Machine Guns.		
Heading	War Diary 127th Machine Gun Company Period 1st June 1917 To 30th June 1917 Vol 5		
War Diary	Havrincourt Wood	01/06/1917	30/06/1917
Map	Appendix I		
Miscellaneous	O No. 9 By 2lt G.w. Barnett Comdg 127 M.g Coy Appendix II	08/06/1917	08/06/1917
Map	Appendix II		
Heading	War Diary Of 127th Machine Gun Company From 1st July 1917 To 31st July 1917 Volume VII		
Map	War Diary Ref 57c Enlarged Is 1/10		
War Diary	Q.1.a.37 Havrincourt Wood	01/07/1917	02/07/1917
War Diary	Havrincourt Wood	03/07/1917	07/07/1917
War Diary	Ruyaulcourt	08/07/1917	09/07/1917
War Diary	Barastre	10/07/1917	10/07/1917
War Diary	Achiet-Le-Petit	11/07/1917	31/07/1917
Heading	War Diary Of 127 Machine Gun Company Period 1st August 1917 To 31st August 1917 Vol 7		
War Diary	Achiet Le Petit	01/08/1917	21/08/1917
War Diary	Aveluy	22/08/1917	22/08/1917
War Diary	Hopoutre	23/08/1917	31/08/1917
Heading	War Diary Of 127th Machine Gun Company Period 1st September 1917 To 30th September 1917 Volume IX		
War Diary	Brandhoek	01/09/1917	06/09/1917
War Diary	Ypres	07/09/1917	14/09/1917

War Diary	Brandhoek	15/09/1917	19/09/1917
War Diary	Hopoutre	20/09/1917	20/09/1917
War Diary	Oudezeele	21/09/1917	22/09/1917
War Diary	Coxyde	23/09/1917	25/09/1917
War Diary	Nieuport Bains	26/09/1917	30/09/1917
Diagram etc	Disposition of Guns for Attack Appendix I		
Diagram etc	Disposition of Guns for Defence 12/9/17 Appendix 2		
Diagram etc	Disposition of Guns for Defence Appendix 3		
War Diary	Nieuport Bains	01/10/1917	07/10/1917
War Diary	Coxyde	09/10/1917	21/10/1917
War Diary	Nieuport	22/10/1917	31/10/1917
Miscellaneous	127th M.G. Coy. Defence Orders.		
Miscellaneous			
Map	Appendix II Disposition of Machine Guns Lombarizyde Sector		
Heading	War Diary Of 127th Machine Gun Company Period 1st October 1917 To 31st October 1917 Vol X		
Heading	War Diary Of 127th Machine Gun Company Period 1st November 1917 To 30th November 1917 Vol 10		
War Diary	Nieuport	31/10/1917	07/11/1917
War Diary	Coxyde	08/11/1917	16/11/1917
War Diary	Teteghem	17/11/1917	17/11/1917
War Diary	Normhoudt	18/11/1917	18/11/1917
War Diary	Hardifort	19/11/1917	19/11/1917
War Diary	Staple Area	20/11/1917	20/11/1917
War Diary	Berguette	21/11/1917	25/11/1917
War Diary	Berguette Coxyde	26/11/1917	27/11/1917
War Diary	Corre	28/11/1917	28/11/1917
War Diary	Givenchy Sector	29/11/1917	01/12/1917
Map	Appendix I Distribution Of Machine Guns Givenchy Sector		
Heading	War Diary Of 127 Machine Gun Company Period 1st December To 31st December 1917 Volume XII		
War Diary	Givenchy Sector	01/12/1917	23/12/1917
War Diary	Bethune	24/12/1917	27/12/1917
War Diary	Essars	28/12/1917	31/12/1917
Heading	War Diary Of 127th Machine Gun Company Period 1st January 1918 To 31st January 1918 Volume I 4 Pages.		
War Diary	Essars	01/01/1918	03/01/1918
War Diary	Givenchy Right Sector	04/01/1918	30/01/1918
War Diary	Essars	31/01/1918	31/01/1918
Map	Part Of Sheet 36c N.W. I		
Heading	War Diary Of 127 Machine Gun Company Period 1st February 1918 To 28th February 1918 Volume II		
War Diary	Essars	01/02/1918	12/02/1918
War Diary	Labeuvriere	13/02/1918	28/02/1918

WO 95/2661 (3)
127 INF BDE
BDE MGC
Mar '17 - Feb '18

42ND DIVISION
127TH INFY BDE

127TH MACHINE GUN COY.
MAR 1917-FEB 1918.

SECRET

Vol II

War Diary

127 Machine Gun Company

Period:- 1st March 1917 to 31st March 1917

Vol III

Army Form C. 2118.

WAR DIARY
INTELLIGENCE SUMMARY

(Erase heading not required.)

127th Machine Gun Company

Sheet 1

Instructions regarding War Diaries and Intelligence Summaries are contained in F. S. Regs., Part II. and the Staff Manual respectively. Title Pages will be prepared in manuscript.

Place	Date	Hour	Summary of Events and Information	Remarks and references to Appendices
			Reference Maps:- 1/100,000 ABBEVILLE 19	
			1/100,000 DIEPPE 16	
			1/100,000 AMIENS 17	
ALEXANDRIA	1.3.17		Arrived ALEXANDRIA 06.30 and embarked on H.M.T. CORSICAN	JH.
- "" -	2.3.17	0900	Sailed from ALEXANDRIA	JH.
H.M.T. CORSICAN	3.3.17		At Sea	JH.
- "" -	4.3.17		- "" -	JH.
- "" -	5.3.17		- "" -	JH.
- "" -	6.3.17		- "" -	JH.
- "" -	7.3.17		- "" -	JH.
- "" -	8.3.17		- "" -	JH.
MARSEILLES	9.3.17		Arrived MARSEILLES and disembarked 4.0 p.m. Entrained 5.45 p.m.	JH.
	10.3.17		In train en route for PONT REMY.	JH.
	11.3.17		Arrived PONT REMY 7.30 p.m. and proceeded to VAUX-MARQUENNEVILLE by march route	JH.
VAUX.	12.3.17	2.50 AM	Arrived at billets at VAUX-MARQUENNEVILLE. Allotting and cleaning of billets. Transport details, having drawn all 1st Line Transport from No 2 Section, A.S.C. A.H.T.D. rejoined Unit	JH.

Army Form C. 2118.

WAR DIARY
or
INTELLIGENCE SUMMARY
(Erase heading not required.)

127th MACHINE GUN COMPANY

Sheet 2.

Place	Date	Hour	Summary of Events and Information	Remarks and references to Appendices
VAUX	13.3.17		Equipping of Unit with VICKER'S guns and gun-equipment	J.H.
"	14.3.17		Physical Training & short route march	J.H.
"	15.3.17		- do -	J.H.
"	16.3.17		- do - 9 M.G and Revolver Instruction, short route march.	J.H.
"	17.3.17		- do - short route march. Advance Party, 1 Officer & 3 O.R. returned from the trenches, having been attached to the 1st Division. One Officer and 2 O.R. proceeded to 1st Machine Gun Company for experience in trench warfare	J.H.
"	18.3.17		Parades for Divine Service	J.H.
"	19.3.17		Physical Training, short route march and M.G. Training	J.H.
"	20.3.17		- do -	J.H.
"	21.3.17		- do -	J.H.
"	22.3.17		- do - and bathing parade. The party, which proceeded on 17th inst. to be temporarily attached to 1st Machine Gun Company, rejoined	J.H.
"	23.3.17		Physical Training, Close Order Drill and M.G. Training	J.H.
"	24.3.17		Physical Training, Mechanism of the gun, and construction of 30yds. range.	J.H.
"	25.3.17		Parades for Divine Service	J.H.

Army Form C. 2118.

WAR DIARY
INTELLIGENCE SUMMARY

127 MACHINE GUN COMPANY

Sheet 3

(Erase heading not required.)

Place	Date	Hour	Summary of Events and Information	Remarks and references to Appendices
VAUX	26.3.17		Physical Training, M.G. and Revolver Firing, Short Route March	J.H.
-"-	27.3.17		-do- -do- Mechanism and Belt-filling	J.H.
-"-	28.3.17		Orders were received to proceed to CHUIGNES. Transport, consisting of 1 Officer, 37 other ranks, 11 riding horses and 46 light draught horses, 13 limbered G.S. Wagons, 1 Water Cart, 1 Cook's Cart, proceeded by march route at 7.30 A.M. The Company, less transport, marched to FONTAINE-SUR-SOMME, marching out 6 Officers, 123 other ranks. Marched out 10.30 A.M. Arrived 2.15 P.M. Distance 15 Kilometres. Casualties:- 2. who rejoined within two hours after the Company reached Lillers, FONTAINE-SUR-SOMME.	J.H.
FONTAINE-SUR-SOMME	29.3.17	8 A.M.	The Company, strength as above, proceeded by rail from PONT-REMY Station to CHUIGNES. Arrived CHUIGNES at 1.15 P.M. and were placed in hutments in MARLY CAMP	J.H.
CHUIGNES	30.3.17		Training. Cleaning of camp	J.H.
-"-	31.3.17		Training. Short route march.	J.H.

D. Hayes. Lieut
Comdg 127 Machine Gun Company.

Confidential　　　　　**Original**

127th Machine Gun Company

War Diary

Period:- 1st April 1917 to 30th April 1917

Vol: IV

Army Form C. 2118.
Original

127 Machine Gun Company

Sheet 1.

WAR DIARY
or
INTELLIGENCE SUMMARY

(Erase heading not required.)

Instructions regarding War Diaries and Intelligence Summaries are contained in F.S. Regs., Part II. and the Staff Manual respectively. Title Pages will be prepared in manuscript.

Place	Date	Hour	Summary of Events and Information	Remarks and references to Appendices
			REFERENCE MAPS :- 1/40,000. FRANCE 62C. 1/20,000 62C N.E.	
			1/40,000 FRANCE 62D 1/20,000 57C S.E.	
HUIGNES	1.4.17		Voluntary Parades for Divine Service. Fitting of Box Respirators.	/a
"	2.4.17		Physical Training, Route March, M.G. Training	/a
"	3.4.17		— do — — do —	/a
"	4.4.17		— do — M.G. Training	/a
"	5.4.17		— do — Route March, Belt-Filling, Bathing Parade.	/a
"	6.4.17		— do — Route March.	/a
"	7.4.17		— do — Inspections of machine-guns and gun-equipment, mechanism	/a
"	8.4.17		Voluntary Parades for Divine Service. Orders were received to proceed to DOMPIERRE	/a
"	9.4.17		The Company, less transport, moved to DOMPIERRE, marching out :- 8 Officers 160 other ranks. Marched out 12.15 p.m. Arrived 2.0 p.m. Distance 6 Kilometres	/a
DOMPIERRE	10.4.17		Overhauling guns and equipment. Clearing up and improving billets	/a
"	11.4.17		Physical Training, Route March, Belt Filling	/a

2449 Wt. W14957/M90 750,000 1/16 J.B.C. & A. Forms/C.2118/12.

Army Form C. 2118.

WAR DIARY
or
INTELLIGENCE SUMMARY

(Erase heading not required.)

127 MACHINE GUN COMPANY
Sheet 2

Instructions regarding War Diaries and Intelligence Summaries are contained in F. S. Regs., Part II. and the Staff Manual respectively. Title Pages will be prepared in manuscript.

Place	Date	Hour	Summary of Events and Information	Remarks and references to Appendices
DOMPIERRE	12.4.17		Physical Training, Route March, Squad Arms Drill, Immediate Action	"
	13.4.17		— do — Stripping & Cleaning. Night Work.	"
	14.4.17		— do — Trench Drill, Gas Helmet Drill, Lecture :- "Angles & Theory of Fire"	"
	15.4.17		Voluntary Parades for Divine Service	"
	16.4.17		Physical Training, Route March, Gas Helmet Drill, Lecture.	"
			Orders received to proceed to PERONNE on 18th inst.	
	17.4.17		Physical Training, Route March, Lecture :- "Machine Guns in Defence"	"
	18.4.17		The Company proceeded to PERONNE, marching out :- 8 Officers, 176 other ranks, 7 riding horses, 45 light draught horses, 13 limbered G.S. Wagons, 1 Water Cart, 1 Cook's Cart. Marched out: 10.30 a.m. Arrived 1.15 p.m. Distance 13 kilometres	"
			Casualties :- NIL.	
PERONNE	19.4.17		Repairing roads and buildings in PERONNE	"
	20.4.17		— do — — do —	"
	21.4.17		— do — — do —	"
	22.4.17		— do — — do —	"
	23.4.17		— do — — do —	"

Army Form C. 2118.

WAR DIARY
or
INTELLIGENCE SUMMARY
(Erase heading not required.)

127 Machine Gun Company.

Sheet 3.

Instructions regarding War Diaries and Intelligence Summaries are contained in F. S. Regs., Part II. and the Staff Manual respectively. Title Pages will be prepared in manuscript.

Place	Date	Hour	Summary of Events and Information	Remarks and references to Appendices
PERONNE.	24.4.17		Repairing roads and buildings in PERONNE	Yes
"	25.4.17		— do — — do —	Yes
"	26.4.17		— do — — do —	Yes
"	27.4.17		— do — — do —	Yes
"	28.4.17		Repairing roads and buildings in PERONNE. Orders were received to relieve 126 Machine Gun Company in the line. Arrangements were made to relieve right subsector on 29th inst. and the left subsector on the 30th inst. Preparations were made for the move.	Yes
"	29.4.17		Advanced Coy. Headquarters. Nos 1 and 3 Sections marched out from PERONNE 8.0 am Yes. Strengths:- Advanced Coy. Headquarters :- 1 Officer, 6 O.R. No 1. Section :- 1 Officer, 25. O.R. No 3 Section :- 1 Officer 24 O.R., 5 G.S. limbered wagons, 27 Horses. Transport returned the same day. Arrangements were made with O.C. 149th Machine Gun Company, occupying sector on the right, for co-operation between guns. No. 3 Section relieved the BROWN LINE in the right subsector at 3.0. P.M. Gun positions were taken up at :- F.8.b.64; F.8.b.46; F.2.a.82; F.1.b.62. No.1. Section relieved the front line in the right subsector at 11.0 P.M. Gun positions were taken up at :- F.5.a.45; X.28.d.16; X.28.a.88; X.27.c.90; The relief was carried out quietly and without any casualties. Complete night reconnaissance, with O.C. 474 Field Coy, R.E., was made of the front defensive line known as the GREEN LINE.	

Army Form C. 2118.

127 MACHINE GUN COMPANY

Sheet 1.

WAR DIARY or INTELLIGENCE SUMMARY

(Erase heading not required.)

Place	Date	Hour	Summary of Events and Information	Remarks and references to Appendices
PERONNE	30.9.17		The Company less Advanced Headquarters & No.s 1 and 3 Sections, moved out from PERONNE 8 P.M. arriving PEIZIERE 12.45 P.M. Distance 20 Kilos. Strengths :- Coy Headquarters :- 1 Officer, 20 O.R. No.2 Section :- 1 Officer, 25 O.R. No.4 Section :- 1 Officer, 24 O.R. Transport Section, 2 Officers, 33 O.R. 53 horses, 13 G.S. limbered wagons, 1 Water Cart, 1 brooks Cart. Headquarters were taken over at 1.30 P.M. No.2 Section relieved the BROWN LINE in the left sub-sector at 2.30 P.M. Gun positions :- F.1.b.19; X.25.c.64; X.25.a.94; X.25.a.25. Disposition of machine guns and Lewis guns for defence of front line was arranged with O.C. 1/6th MANCHESTER RGT., O.C. 1/7th MANCHESTER RGT., occupying front line, and O.C. 474th Field Coy. R.E. Evening reconnaissance was made of night sector GREEN LINE & No.4 Section relieved the front line in the left subsector at midnight. Gun positions were taken up at :- X.22.c.64; X.21.b.95; X.21.c.75; X.21.a.25. The relief was carried out quietly and without casualties. Strengths in the line :- No.1 Section :- 1 Officer, 25 O.R. No.3 Section :- 1 Officer, 24 O.R. No.2 Section :- 1 Officer, 25 O.R. No.4 Section :- 1 Officer, 24 O.R. Company Headquarters :- 2 Officers, 21 O.R. Transport and reserve gunners :- 2 Officers, 29 O.R.	X

H Aldous Major

Cmdg. 127th Machine Gun Company

CONFIDENTIAL

VOLUME V

War Diary

of

127th Machine Gun Company.

Period :— 1st May 1917 to 31st May 1917

Army Form C. 2118

127 Machine Gun Company
Sheet No. 1

WAR DIARY
or
INTELLIGENCE SUMMARY
(Erase heading not required.)

Instructions regarding War Diaries and Intelligence Summaries are contained in F. S. Regs, Part II. and the Staff Manual respectively. Title Pages will be prepared in manuscript.

Place	Date	Hour	Summary of Events and Information	Remarks and references to Appendices
PEIZIÉRES			REFERENCE MAPS:- 57C S.E. 1/20000, 57C N.E. 1/20000, 62C N.E. 1/20000.	
	1/5/17		Reconnaissance of BROWN LINE. Disposition of machine guns and Lewis Guns settled with O.C. 474th Field Coy R.E. Night reconnaissance made of GREEN LINE with G.O.C. 127th Infantry Brigade; R.E. Officers and Corps Officers for purpose of deciding upon a system of strong localities. During this reconnaissance the G.O.C. 127th Infantry Brigade was killed.	J.C.
	2/5/17		New emplacements in BROWN LINE completed and dug-outs commenced.	J.C.
	3/5/17		Work continued on emplacements and dug-outs in GREEN LINE and BROWN LINE. Re disposition of guns in left sector of GREEN LINE to conform with newly sited localities. His Majesty the King has been pleased to approve the award of the Distinguished Conduct Medal to the following Warrant Officer of this unit:- 10916 A/C.S.M. A.A. HESTER. For acts of gallantry and devotion to duty in the field. (EXTRACT. LONDON GAZETTE a/26.4.17)	J.C.

Army Form C. 2118

127th Machine Gun Company
Sheet No 2

WAR DIARY
or
INTELLIGENCE SUMMARY
(Erase heading not required.)

Place	Date	Hour	Summary of Events and Information	Remarks and references to Appendices
PEIZIÉRES	4/5/17		Construction of emplacements and dug-outs. Re-disposition of guns and men completed.	(appendix I)
	5/5/17		Brigade conference on disposition for the GREEN LINE.	
	6/5/17	6 A.M.	At 6 A.M. GREEN LINE taken over as main line of defence. Two guns arranged for indirect fire on Ossus, road from Ossus to point X 30 A 87, also roads and reported positions in vicinity. Fire was not opened owing to very strong wind, rendering long range fire unreliable.	
	7/5/17		Construction of emplacements and dug-outs in GREEN and BROWN LINES proceeded with.	
	8/5/17		Work proceeded with on emplacements and dug-outs in GREEN and BROWN LINES. Indirect fire was opened at 3 A.M. to 4 A.M. and 8 A.M. to 9 A.M. on to:- (1) OSSUS; (2) road from OSSUS to OSSUS WOOD; (3) road running south of OSSUS WOOD as far as point X 30 A 88; (4) northeast half of OSSUS WOOD. A German machine gun was reported to be in far end of OSSUS WOOD and a gun was laid to open fire on it. However the hostile gun fired on our aircraft. Relief of BROWN LINE, right subsector, was carried out to-day. The relief was completed by 5 P.M. No 1 Section moved down to rest at LONGAVESNES on relief.	

Army Form C. 2118

127th MACHINE GUN COMPANY

Sheet No. 3.

WAR DIARY
or
INTELLIGENCE SUMMARY
(Erase heading not required.)

Place	Date	Hour	Summary of Events and Information	Remarks and references to Appendices
PEIZIÈRES.	9/5/17		Relief of GREEN LINE right subsector by section of 125th Company was completed by 2 A.M. No. 3 Section moved down to rest at LONGAVESNES, arriving 4.30 A.M. The 125th Company took over remaining positions of left subsector BROWN LINE at 4.30 p.m., completing relief of BROWN LINE.	JL
	10/5/17		Relief of the left subsector GREEN LINE, by the 125th Company, completing the relief of the whole company, was finished by 1.15 A.M. The relief was carried out in good order, quietly and without any casualties. Pack animals were used to carry the guns from Nos 5, 6, 7 and 8 positions in the GREEN LINE and were found to be very useful.	JL
			The guns and equipment were overhauled, cleaned and checked.	JH
LONGAVESNES			It has been found, during this first tour of duty in the trenches in France, that a fighting section of 1 Officer and 26 O.R. is about the right strength to send in the line; all the surplus gunners being kept at Company H.Q. and transport lines in order to replace casualties.	JL

Army Form C. 2118

127th Machine Gun Company

Sheet 4

WAR DIARY
INTELLIGENCE SUMMARY
(Erase heading not required.)

Place	Date	Hour	Summary of Events and Information	Remarks and references to Appendices
LONGAVESNES	10/5/17		The men in the line report that the rationing had been very good and suggestions were made, by Section Officers, as to its further improvement. A conference was held of all officers at 6 p.m. to discuss the lessons learnt and also to make arrangements for the next tour of duty.	JH
	11/5/17		Company training proceeded with; close order drill, rifle exercises and machine gun training. In the afternoon the Company witnessed an exhibition given by the 127th Light Trench Mortar Battery at J6.b.33, where the value of the 3" Stokes Gun was demonstrated.	JH
	12/5/17		Company training proceeded with; close order drill, rifle exercises, machine gun training and bombing instruction.	JH

Army Form C. 2118.

127th Machine Gun Company

Sheet No. 5.

WAR DIARY
or
INTELLIGENCE SUMMARY
(Erase heading not required.)

Place	Date	Hour	Summary of Events and Information	Remarks and references to Appendices
LONG AVESNES	13/5/17		Church Parade.	J.L.
	14/5/17		Company training; 25 yds range practice.	J.L.
	15/5/17		Company training; bombing, machine gun training, practice on 25 yds range.	J.L.
	16/5/17		25 yds range practice, A German machine gun issued to the company was fired and instruction given on it.	J.L.
	17/5/17		The Company proceeded by Route March to NEUVILLE – BOURJONVAL, Marching out 6 A.M. Arrived 11.30 A.M. Distance 17 Kilos, Casualties: Nil. Strength marching out :– 6 Officers; 186 O.R. 48 Horses, 13 G.S.L. Wagons. 1 water cart and 1 cook's cart.	J.H.
NEUVILLE	18/5/17 & 19/5/17		Cleaning up guns, equipment and billets. Reconnaissance by C.O. and Officers Commanding Nos 1 and 2 Sections, of the front line held by 61st Machine Gun Company. Relief commenced by the 61st Company in the line. Positions A 1, 2, 3 and 4. C 1, 2, 3 and 4 were taken over by Nos 1 and 2 Sections. Relief of these two sections commenced 9 p.m. and completed by 11.30 p.m. (18th inst) No. 3 and 4 Sections, less 1/2 Section, relieved remainder of 61st Company in the line and reserve line. Positions B 1, 3 and 4. D 1, 2 and 3. Relief commenced 9 p.m. and completed by 10.30 p.m. (19th inst).	J.L. J.H.

1875. Wt. W593/826 1,000,000 4/15 J.B.C. & A. A.D.S.S./Forms/C. 2118.

Army Form C. 2118

127th Machine Gun Company

Sheet No. 6.

WAR DIARY
or
INTELLIGENCE SUMMARY
(Erase heading not required.)

Instructions regarding War Diaries and Intelligence Summaries are contained in F.S. Regs., Part II. and the Staff Manual respectively. Title Pages will be prepared in manuscript.

Place	Date	Hour	Summary of Events and Information	Remarks and references to Appendices
NEUVILLE	18/19/4/5/17		Pack animals were used throughout this relief in taking up and bringing back guns and ammunition, and the value of training all animals to pack was emphasized.	J.L.
RUYAULCOURT	20/5/17		H.Q. of 61st Company at PLOC Central taken over at 11 a.m.	J.L.
	20/5/17		Improving positions. Fresh dug-outs commenced.	J.L.
	21/5/17		Lieut. ELLIOTT with ½ Section proceeded to HAUT-ALLAINES (62c I5) as anti-aircraft guard to XV Corps H.Q.	J.L.
			Positions and dug-outs improved. A thorough reconnaissance of the line was made with a view to reorganising.	J.L.
	22/5/17		O.C. Company accompanied B.G. Cmdg 127th INFANTRY BRIGADE in a reconnaissance of the line, when fresh gun positions were fixed and agreed upon together with team gun positions.	J.L. (appendix II)
	23/5/17	9 p.m.	Re-organisation of line commenced. A composite section was formed of half section No 1 Section and one detachment from No 1 Section. Composite Section returned to Company Hd Qrs to rest.	J.L.
			No 1 Section less one detachment, and No 2 Section took over gun positions in the front, support and reserve lines. No 3 Section in reserve with H.Q. at HUBERT'S CROSS and with guns in position in the intermediate line.	J.L.
	24/5/17		Work proceeded with, completing new emplacements and improving old ones.	J.L.

WAR DIARY
INTELLIGENCE SUMMARY

(Erase heading not required.)

Army Form C. 2118.

127th Machine Gun Company

Sheet No. 7

Place	Date	Hour	Summary of Events and Information	Remarks and references to Appendices
	25/5/17		No. 3 Section relieved No. 2 Section in the firing line. Work proceeded with, completing emplacements and constructing dug-outs.	JH.
	26/5/17		Composite section relieved No. 1 Section in the front line. No. 1 Section returning to Company H.Q. to rest.	JH.
	27/5/17		Completing emplacements and dug outs.	JH.
	28/5/17		Reconnaissance of the line by O.C. Company with Divisional and Corps Machine Gun officers to fix approximate line for indirect and covering fire. Work was proceeded with improving emplacements and dug outs.	JH.
	29/5/17		The line was reorganised on reaching over the right battalion sector to 126th INFANTRY BRIGADE. No. 2 section relieved position at K 32 c 66; K 32 a 72; K 31 d 26 and occupied a new position at K 32 a 24.; No. 3 section (3 teams) returning to the intermediate line.	Appendix III
			A conference of C.O's with B.G. Comdg. 127 INFANTRY BRIGADE was held at 1/5 MANCHESTER REGT's H.Q. at P 18 B 3 8, when the future policy was discussed.	JH.
	30/5/17		Direct fire was opened on chalk pit near cross roads K 33 b 17, by a gun placed out in the open, approximately I 32 c 37. Fire was kept up from 8.30 p.m. to 11 p.m. to assist a patrol from the 1/8 MANCHESTER REGT who were making a reconnaissance of the point K 33 b 11.	JH.

Army Form C. 2118.

127 Machine Gun Coy
Sheet N° 8.

WAR DIARY
or
INTELLIGENCE SUMMARY
(Erase heading not required.)

Place	Date	Hour	Summary of Events and Information	Remarks and references to Appendices
	30/5/17		Three guns from No 1 Section took over new position at Q 2 d 92 and relieved composite section positions at Q 2 d 85 65 and Q 2 d 79, the remaining teams of No 3 Section returning to position Q 2 d 13. All reliefs were carried out quietly and without casualties.	JH.
	31/5/17		Reconnaissance of reserve line to select probable machine gun positions. Orders were received to place as many guns as possible to assist parts to force their way into points K 34 c 29; K 34 d 20; Copse at K 33 b 65; K 33 central. Five machine guns were placed in suitable positions and fire was opened at 11 p.m. Points fired on were:— Road junction K 33 c 70; K 33 a 70 15; K 34 a 45 05; K 34 at 5500. and a search was made of all ground north of Illies.	JH.
			Appendices:-
I. Disposition of guns and wire in BROWN LINE.
II. Disposition of Machine Guns and Lewis Guns etc. ammunition.
III. Disposition of Machine Gun preparatory to handing over of right battalion sector.	JH.

J Hayes. LIEUT.
CMDG. 127TH MACHINE GUN COY

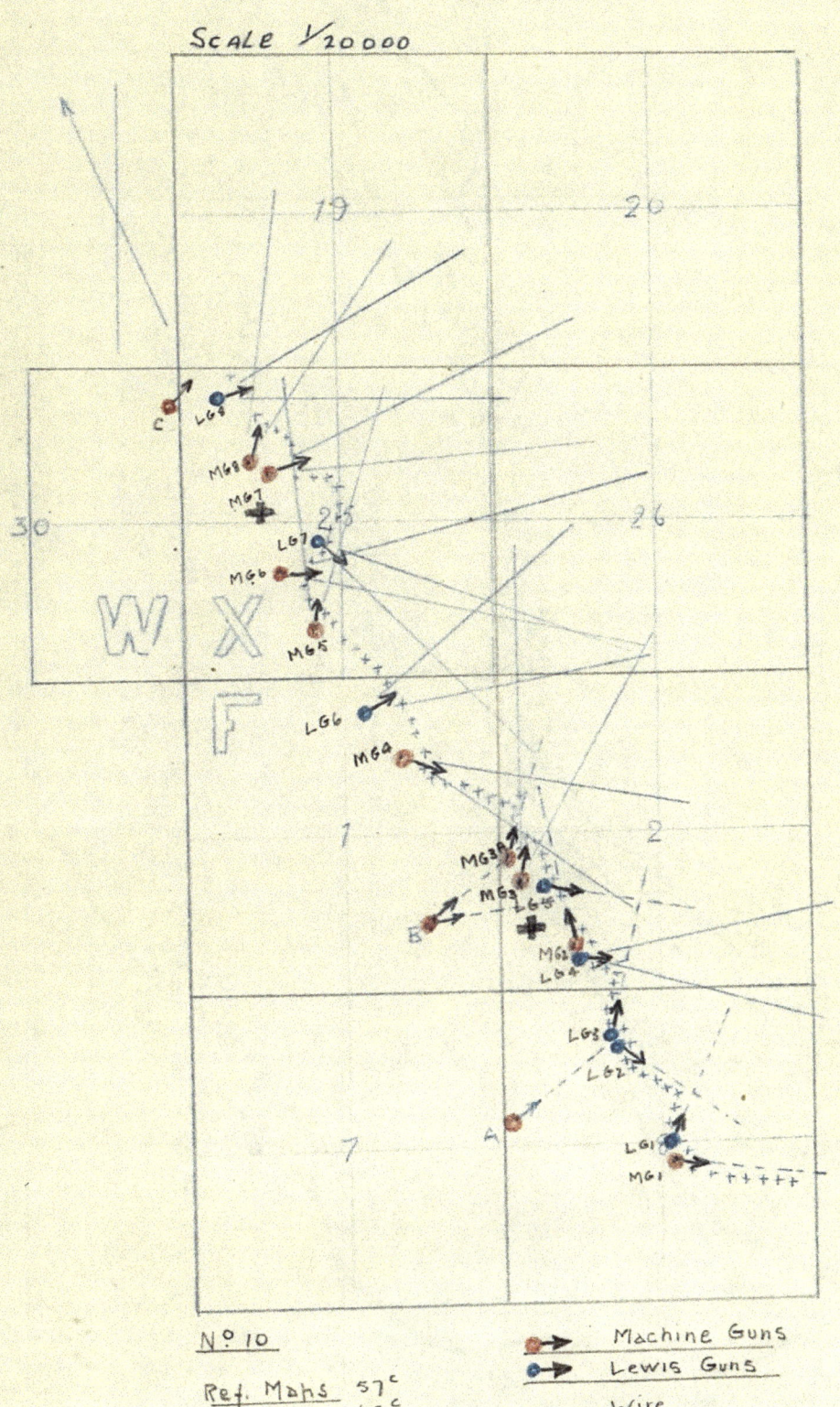

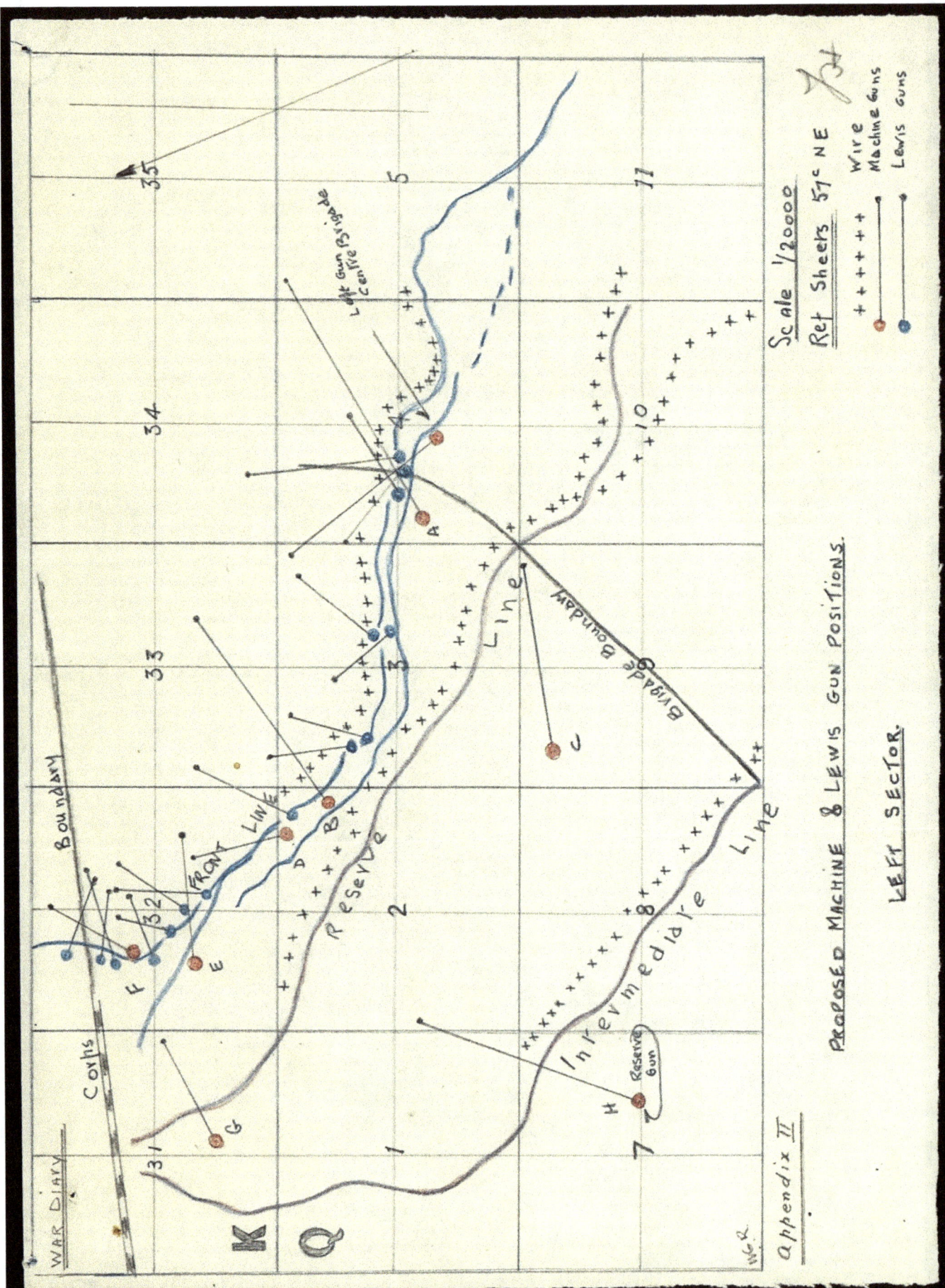

Appendix III

Position of Machine Guns
after re-organisation

● ———→ Machine Guns
+ + + + + + + Wire
Map Ref:- 57c

Volume 6   Confidential

Vol 5

War Diary

127th. Machine Gun Company.

Period :- 1st. June 1917 to 30th. June 1917.

Army Form C.2118.

WAR DIARY or INTELLIGENCE SUMMARY

(Erase heading not required.)

121st Machine Gun Coy.
Sheet No. 1

Place	Date	Hour	Summary of Events and Information	Remarks and references to Appendices
Havrincourt Wood	1.6.17		Ref. Maps:- 57^d N.E. 1/20000. 57^d S.E. The firing commenced on night of May 31st was continued, and at 1 a.m. fire was lifted to North of the line :- Cross Roads K.33.c.9.0.85 to the road junction K.34.c.3.6. At 1.4 a.m. fire was lifted North of the line - cross roads K.33.b.1.4 - K.34. Central. The enemy commenced shelling at 1.10 a.m. and appeared to be searching for the guns. Two guns which had been placed in Water Cohse ceased fire immediately as shells dropping near them. The remainder kept up intermittent bursts of fire until 1.40 a.m. Ammunition expended:- 10,380 Rounds. Casualties:- 1 Officer (2Lt. A.J. Ferguson) and 1 O.R. (No 48010 L/Cpl J. Robinson) both slightly wounded and remained at duty. Very few stoppages occurred, all the guns firing well. It was not possible to observe the fire.	J.H.
	1/2.6.17		A and C positions were relieved by the 126th Coy at midnight. These two teams returned to the Intermediate line and relieved No.3 section. No 3 section retired to Coy H.Q.rs to rest.	J.H.
	2/3.6.17 3.6.17 4.6.17		Work on gun positions and dugouts proceeded with. Casualties: 1 O.R. (201350 Pte J. Jennings) Wounded (to hospital) Four unknown fire positions constructed and punk holes made. Casualties:- 1 O.R. (59986 Pte J Bowen) wounded and remained at duty. (Appendix I)	J.H.

Army Form C. 2118.

127 Machine Gun Company

Sheet No. 2

WAR DIARY or INTELLIGENCE SUMMARY

(Erase heading not required.)

Place	Date	Hour	Summary of Events and Information	Remarks and references to Appendices
	5.6.17		Company Headquarters were established at P.2.c.2.2. Work on emplacements and dugouts continued.	JH
	6.6.17		Positions and dugouts completed and communication trenches improved.	JH
	7/8.6.17		Indirect fire was carried out on to K26d, K27 and K21b, (from forward positions) to support the attack by the 145th Company. Positions and dugouts improved.	JH
	8.6.17		Orders were issued by Brigade for the infantry to establish a line approximately:- K33c 70 to K32 b.2.1. and K32 b.17 to K32 a.99. Machine Guns in position in front line were laid ready to open fire should the digging and covering parties be forced to retire. (Appendix I)	JH
	9.6.17		Digging again took place during the night, our Machine Guns, together with those of the 145 Company being laid for covering fire to protect the digging party in case of enemy attack. New positions were improved and communication trenches dug.	JH
	10.6.17		Work on new positions and dugouts proceeded with.	JH
	11/12.6.17		Indirect fire, in conjunction with Artillery, was carried out from Indirect Fire position, by two guns from Intermediate Line and the guns from G and H positions on to the Crater and Dopsloo at end of Slag Heap from 11.30pm to 12.40am. Enemy retaliated with minenwerfers on to the Slag Heap.	JH
	13.6.17		The team occupying K position (new position in F post) was withdrawn. Work on new positions and communication trenches proceeded with.	JH
	13/14.6.17		The Brigade Front was reorganised, the 126th Company taking over A and B positions. No 1 Section taking over C position. No 4 Section returned to transport lines to rest. The four guns in the Indirect Fire position carried out indirect fire on to valley K33b to K34a from 1.46am to 1.50am.	JH

Army Form C. 2118.

127 Machine Gun Company
Sheet No 2

WAR DIARY or INTELLIGENCE SUMMARY

(Erase heading not required.)

Place	Date	Hour	Summary of Events and Information	Remarks and references to Appendices
	14.6.17		Company Headquarters moved to new position Q.1.a.3.7.	M.
	15/16.6.17		No 2 Section relieved No 3 Section in Right Subsector. No 3 Section remaining at Left Subsector H.Qrs to be available for indirect fire and Barrage work.	M.
	17.6.17		At 9.30 p.m. No 3 Section moved to positions in the Intermediate Line. Section H.Qrs being established at Company H.Qrs.	M.
	18/19.6.17		No 4 Section relieved No 1 Section in G and H positions, the two remaining teams proceeding to Left Section H.Qrs to be available for indirect fire.	M.
			No 1 Section returned to Transport Lines to rest. Indirect fire was carried out from the four Indirect Fire positions to Zouap Valley K.33.b.02 to K.34.a.52 commencing at 11 p.m. The guns were withdrawn at 2 a.m. owing to heavy hostile shelling. Work on the front line positions commenced. Emplacements and dug-outs in the Intermediate Line improved.	
	20.6.17			M.
	21.6.17		The Front Line defence guns were allotted as follows:—	M.
			Right Subsector C, D, and H positions	
			Left Subsector E, F and G positions	
			Indirect Fire guns:— one gun per Section from Right Subsector and one gun per Section Left Subsector. These guns to be established at Left Subsection H.Qrs and to be under the command of the Officer i/c Left Subsector.	

Army Form C. 2118.

121 Machine Gun Company

Sheet No 4.

WAR DIARY or INTELLIGENCE SUMMARY
(Erase heading not required.)

Place	Date	Hour	Summary of Events and Information	Remarks and references to Appendices
	21/22.6.17		No. 4 Section took over D position from No. 2 Section, the team relieved returning to Left Subsector H.Q. to be available for Indirect Firing. Work on all positions was proceeded with.	JH
	23/24/6/17		No. 1 Section relieved No. 2 Section. The Teams relieving E.F. and G positions and one team relieving team in Indirect Fire position. Construction of emplacements and dugouts proceeded with.	JH
	24/25.6.17		No. 3 Section relieved No. 4 Section in G.D and H positions, one team Indirect Fire position. No. 4 Section taking over positions in the Intermediate Line. Work on new Front Line position and emplacements, and dugouts in the Intermediate Line proceeded with.	JH
	25/26.6.17		Indirect fire was carried out from Indirect Fire positions on to Wood K33c from 9 p.m. until 10.25 p.m. Work was continued on new positions in Front Line and Intermediate Line.	JH
	26/27.6.17		From 9.30 p.m. to 9.40 p.m. and 2.30 am to 2.40 am three guns carried out Indirect fire on to enemy position in K27c, Chalk pit in K33b and Grand Ravine from K33a.35 to K33a.76. Indirect fire was also carried out by two guns on to K26b and K21c from 1.30 am to 2.10 am in support of the 14'5 Company. Work was continued on new positions on Front Line and Intermediate Line.	JH
	27/28.6.17		Indirect fire was again carried out by two guns on to N.E. part of K33c and S.W. part of K27d from 9.15 p.m. to 9.30 p.m. and 2.10 am to 2.30 am. One gun carried out Indirect fire on Vesuvius and track from Vesuvius to K26d.95 from 10 p.m. to 11 p.m. Work to dugouts to emplacements proceeded with and revetting and camouflaging emplacements on North side of Yorkshire Bank.	JH

Army Form C. 2118

127 Machine Gun Company.
Sheet No 5.

WAR DIARY
or
INTELLIGENCE SUMMARY
(Erase heading not required.)

Instructions regarding War Diaries and Intelligence Summaries are contained in F. S. Regs., Part II. and the Staff Manual respectively. Title Pages will be prepared in manuscript.

Place	Date	Hour	Summary of Events and Information	Remarks and references to Appendices
	28/29.6.17		Indirect fire was opened on East end of new Hostile trench K27c0540 from 10.30 pm to 10.5 pm; and also on N.E. part of T33b and S.W. part of K27d from 9.15 pm to 9.45 pm and 1.45 am until 2.45 am. Work was continued on sap between position and dugout on the front side of Yorkshire Bank, and the intermediate line was drained and improved.	JH
	29/30.6.17		No 2 Section relieved No 3 section. Three teams relieving C. D. and H positions and one team relieving the team available for indirect fire, at the left. Section H.Q. No 3 Section returned to Transport Lines to rest. Indirect fire from Indirect fire positions, was opened on to the front Eastern part of K33b and South Western part of K27d commencing at 9.10 pm, with intervals of not more than half an hour, until 3 am. Indirect fire was also opened on ground in the vicinity of Grand Ravine and Chalk Pit in K33b from 10.30 pm until 3 am. Two emplacements damaged by rain, on front side Yorkshire Bank were repaired and position in the intermediate line was improved.	JH
	30.6.17		Indirect fire was opened on North Eastern part of K33G; also on Crater K27d.33 and K27d. Work on communication trenches was continued and dugouts improved.	JH

Appendices:—
I. Sketch showing Indirect fire positions, R position in Front and new Brigade front.
II. A Copy of Orders by O.C. 127th M.G. Coy for the night 8/9th June giving the Coordinates of Machine Guns and Targets. Sketch showing new front line with Machine Gun positions for proposed defence scheme.

Strength:— 10 Officers, transferred.
172 O.R.
26 O.R. attached.

Casualties:— One Officer and Three Other Ranks.
Remarks:— 7 O.R. (One O.R. since died)

J Hayes, Capt.
Cmdg, 127th Machine Gun Company.

1875 Wt. W593/826 1,000,000 4/15 J.B.C. & A./A.D.S.S./Forms/C. 2118.

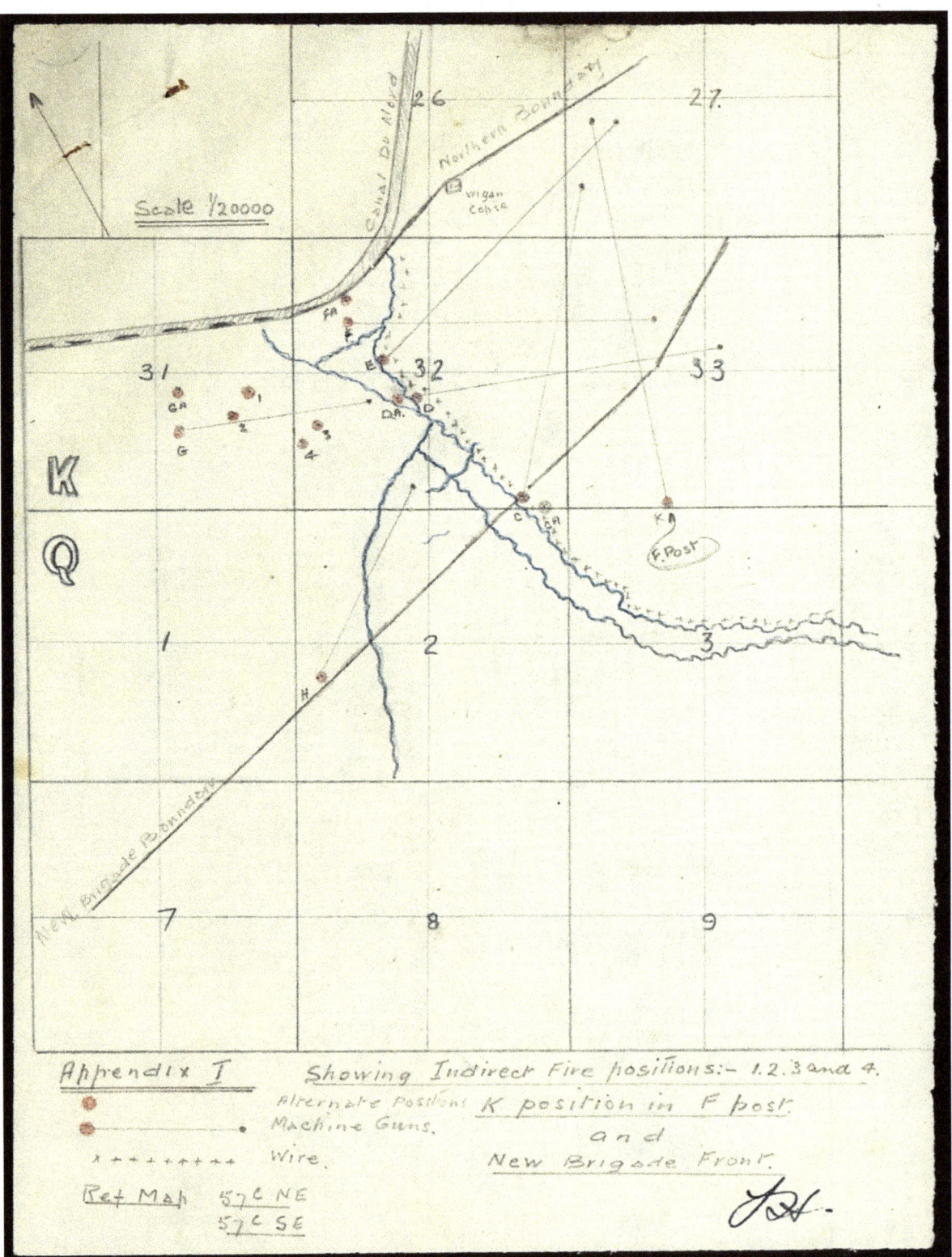

O. No. 9   Appendix II

by 2/Lt J.W. Barrett   8th June 1917.
cmdg. 127 M.G. Coy.

Ref map 1/10000 57c   Brigade Sketch.

I. On the night of 8th/9th June the Brigade will establish a line approximately

     Post F   K33c 70 to K32 b 21
               K32 b 17   K32 a 99.

II. Should the enemy interfere with the work, artillery, machine gun and trench mortar assistance are available on demand to Brigade H.Q.

III. Artillery

18 pounders S.O.S.   line point of wood K33 d 20 35 to copse K32 b 87 inclusive. Howitzers will fire on known hostile M.G. positions.

IV. M.Gs. The 148th Coy. M.G. Corps will fire on the German trenches K26 d 10 95 to K27 c 27. The Machine Guns of the 127th Brigade will be organised as follows:-

1/ Night of June 8th.

(a) All guns in positions in first line of defence will lay on their night lines ready to open fire should the digging and covering parties be forced to retire.

     O.C. Sections will be in close communication with O.C. Sectors and will open fire only when he demands it.

(b) Six guns will carry out indirect overhead fire as below:-

Positions	Coordinates	Targets
1	K32c 0547	Gunpin Wood K34a 44.
2	K32c 1555	" " " K34a 36
3	K31d 5170	" " " K33b 46
4	K31d 5783	Crater K27c 3575
5 } same as	M.G	K27d 3025
6 } 3 and 4	M.G	K33c 65.

These guns will only open fire if called upon for a period of three minutes commencing the next clock 5 minutes but one.

(c) Two guns will be in reserve at Coy H.Q.

V Covering fire in the event of an attack on June 9th

(a) Guns in the line will fire as follows:-

	Position	Target
A Gun	Q2b 79	Road K33b 49.
C "	Q2b 79	" " ".
D "	K32c 66	" K33a 5085
E "	K32a 72	Cross Roads K33c 9085
F.A. "	K32a 72	" " " "

(b) One gun will be in position in F post to command new enemy snipers post etc by "Stand to"

Line of fire 335° Grid.

(c) Indirect fire will be carried out as for the night of June 8th.

(d) Right Sector will have two guns in reserve in usual positions i.e:-

                                    Co-ordinates
    B Gun   Q2b 79
    H "   Q2c 27

Left Sector one gun in reserve i.e:-
    G Gun   K31 d 26.

                                  J.W. Barrett 2/LIEUT.
                              CMDG. 127 Machine Gun Coy.

Copy No. 1   issued to   B.H.Q.
  "   " 2   "   "   1/5 Manchester Regt
  "   " 3   "   "   1/6   "   "
  "   " 4   "   "   1/7   "   "
  "   " 5   "   "   1/8   "   "
  "   " 6   } War Diary.
  "   " 7

Issued by Orderly at 6.p.m.

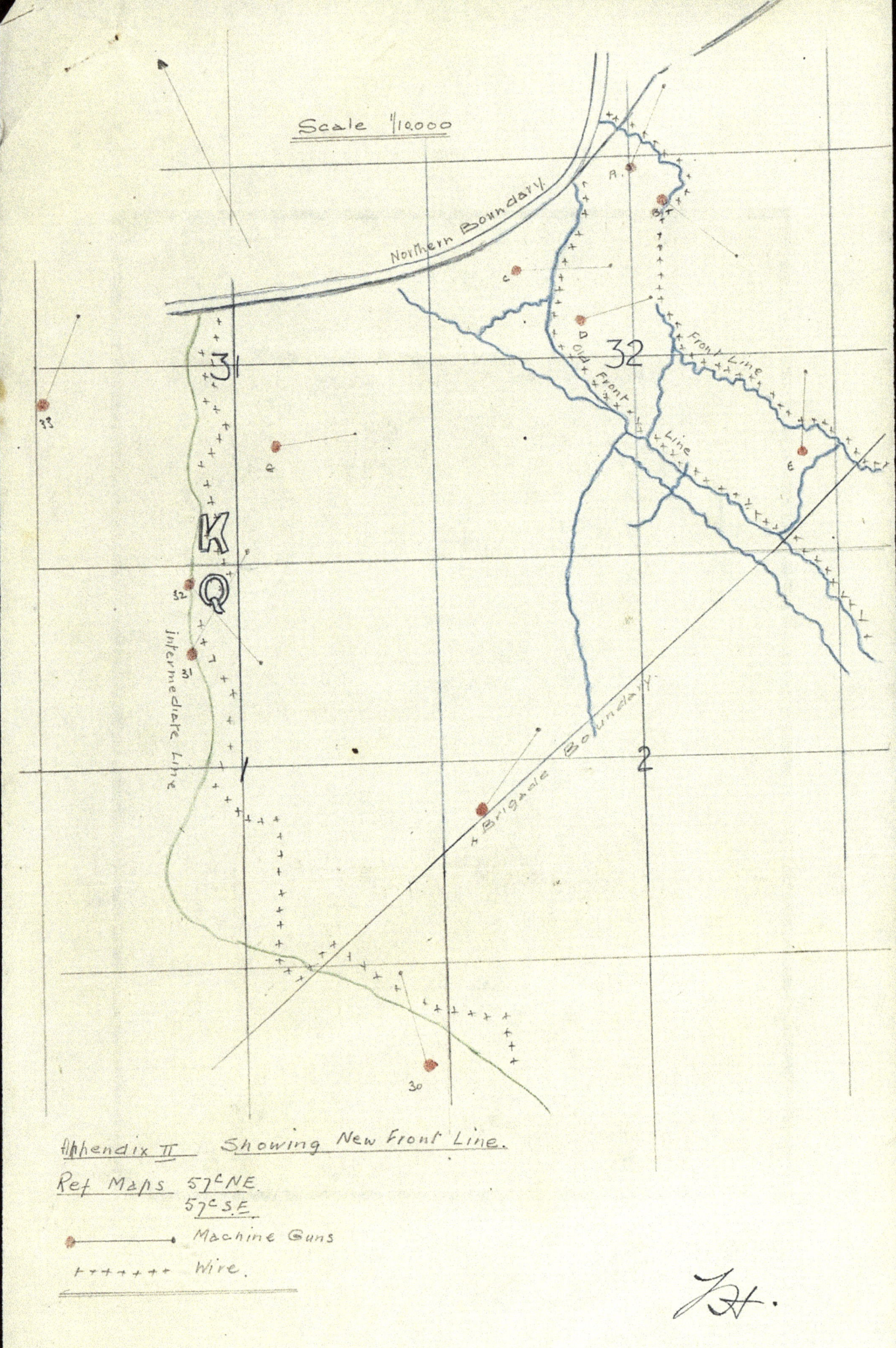

CONFIDENTIAL

Volume VII

War Diary

of

127th Machine Gun Company

From 1st July 1917 to 31st July 1917

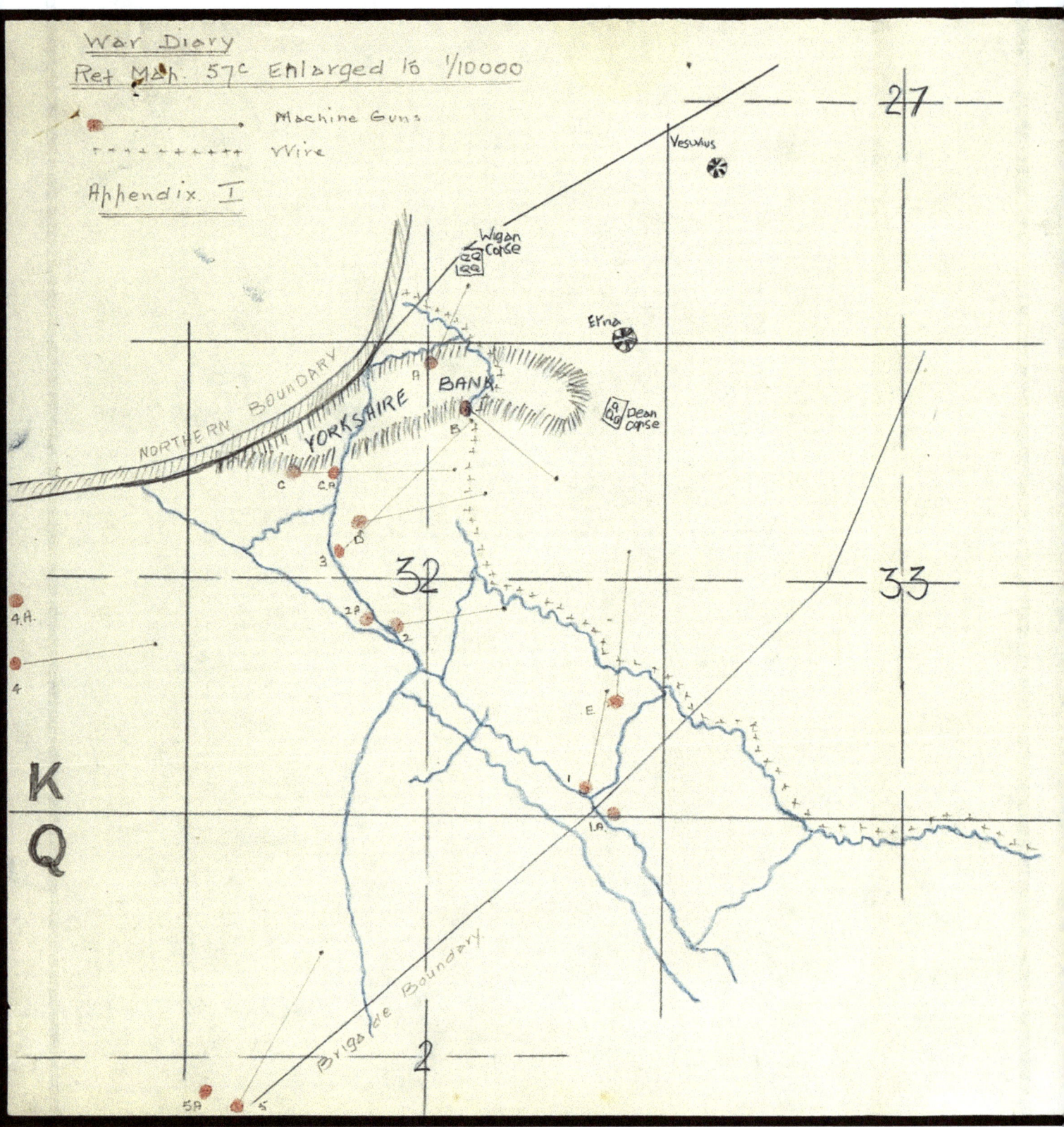

Army Form C. 2118.

WAR DIARY
INTELLIGENCE SUMMARY

127th MACHINE GUN COMPANY
Sheet I

Instructions regarding War Diaries and Intelligence Summaries are contained in F. S. Regs., Part II. and the Staff Manual respectively. Title Pages will be prepared in manuscript.

(Erase heading not required.)

Place	Date	Hour	Summary of Events and Information	Remarks and references to Appendices
Q.1.a.37 HAVRINCOURT WOOD	1/2.7.17		REFERENCE MAPS :- 1/40,000. Sheet 57 C. 1/20,000 Sheets, 57 C. N.E. and S.E.	
			No. 4 Section relieved No. 1 Section, three teams relieving F.F.A. and G. positions and one team relieving the team available for indirect fire, at Left Sub-sector H.Q. No.1. Section took over positions No. 30, 31, 32 & 33, in the Intermediate Line, with Section H.Q. at Coy H.Q. (Q.1.a.37) Indirect fire was opened on the North East part of K33b, on Crater K27.d.33, and on Wood K27.d. from 9.20 p.m. until 11 p.m and from 2.30 a.m. until 3.15 a.m. The new position 'B' at K.32.b.1070 was occupied, and work on emplacement and dugout proceeded with. Communication trenches to positions were drained and deepened.	Yes
	2/3. 7.17		Indirect fire was opened from positions Q.1.a.76 and K.31.d.26 on to Crater K27.d.3525 and on to Track at K.33.b.3075 from 9.30 p.m. until 10.15 p.m. and from 2.15 a.m. until 3 a.m. From 1.8 a.m. until 1.28 a.m. three guns, in conjunction with Artillery and Trench Mortars, opened covering fire for raiding parties of the 1/7th and 1/8th Manchester Regts. Work was proceeded with on all positions and dug-outs.	Yes

2449 Wt. W14957/M90 750,000 1/16 J.B.C. & A. Forms/C.2118/12.

Army Form C. 2118.

127 Machine Gun Coy.

Sheet 2.

WAR DIARY
or
INTELLIGENCE SUMMARY

(Erase heading not required.)

Place	Date	Hour	Summary of Events and Information	Remarks and references to Appendices
HAVRINCOURT WOOD	3/4.7.17		Indirect Fire was opened from positions at Q2c 27, Q1a 76 and K31d 26. on to K27d 3525, K27c 9540 to K27c 9545 and Wood. Fire commenced at 9.10 p.m. until 10 p.m. and from 2 a.m. until 3.15 a.m. Work was continued on new positions off CURLING ALLEY, and on dugout at foot of YORKSHIRE BANK. Emplacements and communication trenches improved.	JGC
-"-	4.7.17		From 3 p.m. until 3.30 p.m. Indirect Fire (ALDOUS METHOD) was opened on to VESUVIUS and tracks and trenches in vicinity. Observations was good and fire was very effective. From 9.30 p.m. with intervals until 10.10 p.m. and 2.45 a.m. with intervals until 3.15 a.m. Indirect Fire was opened on to Area K33b 2580 to K27d 3520 and on area round K27 c 9545 A fatigue party was supplied to assist the R.E.'s to carry timber up for dugouts in the Line. A new emplacement was commenced at approx. K.32.a.80. Dugouts and trenches were improved	JGC
-"-	4/5 7.17		No 3. Section relieved No1. Section, No. 3. Section taking over positions 30. 31. 32 and 33 in the Intermediate Line. No 1. Section returned to Transport Lines to rest.	JGC

Army Form C. 2118.

127 MACHINE Gun Coy

Sheet 3

WAR DIARY
or
INTELLIGENCE SUMMARY

(Erase heading not required.)

Place	Date	Hour	Summary of Events and Information	Remarks and references to Appendices
HAVRINCOURT WOOD.	5/6.7.17.		The guns in the new and old Front lines were re-numbered A.M.G. was placed in Fire Bay 37 (approx. K32 d 2590) and opened direct fire on to DEAN COPSE in co-operation with Artillery and Trench Mortars. Fire commenced at 11.15 p.m. At 11.25 p.m. owing to heavy hostile fire, this gun was withdrawn and placed in Fire Bay 35 (approx. K32 d 2590) where fire was continued until 12.15 A.M. Indirect Fire was opened on trench from K27c.03 to K27c.3020 and along GRAND RAVINE and east end of DEAN COPSE. A fatigue party was supplied to assist the R.E's in carrying up timber for dugouts. Positions were improved and trenches deepened.	APPENDIX I
"	6/7.7.17.		Indirect Fire was opened on to K33 b 2050 and K27 d 4050 from 9.20 p.m. until 10.30 p.m. and 2.10 A.M. until 3 A.M. No. 3. Section were withdrawn from the Intermediate Line and proceeded to the Transport lines at RUYALCOURT. A fatigue party was supplied to assist R.E's in carrying up Timber for dugouts.	
"	7/8.7.17.		The Company was relieved by the 215 Company and returned to rest billets at RUYALCOURT.	

Army Form C. 2118.

127th MACHINE GUN COY

Sheet 4.

WAR DIARY
or
INTELLIGENCE SUMMARY
(Erase heading not required.)

Place	Date	Hour	Summary of Events and Information	Remarks and references to Appendices
RUYALCOURT.	8.7.17		The morning was spent in cleaning and overhauling equipment. At 3p.m. there was an inspection of guns and gun stores by the C.O. The Company paraded for Divine Service at 7p.m.	

	9.7.17.		The morning was spent in packing guns and stores. At 2.50p.m. the Company moved out of billets and proceeded by march route to BARASTRE (CAMP O.16) On arrival, at 5p.m. camp was pitched for the night. Marching out:-
			 Officers. Interpreter. O.R. Horses. Vehicles. Bicycles
			                                                                                  2Wh.
			   8 1 161 52 13 2 2
			 Casualties:- NIL. Distance:- 8 KILOS.	

BARASTRE	10.7.17		At 8.90 a.m. the Company moved off by march route, together with the remainder of the 127th Infantry Brigade Group, en route for ACHIET LE PETIT. The Company arrived at the Camping ground G.19a.19 at 1.40 p.m. Marching out:-
			 Officers. Interpreter. O.R. Horses. Vehicles. Bicycles
			                                                                                   4Wh. 2Wh.
			   8 1 160 52 13 2 4.
			 Casualties:- NIL. Distance:- 18 KILOS.
			 The afternoon was spent in constructing bivouacs and cleaning camp.	

Army Form C. 2118.

WAR DIARY
or
INTELLIGENCE SUMMARY

(Erase heading not required.)

127 Machine Gun Coy.

Sheet 5.

Instructions regarding War Diaries and Intelligence Summaries are contained in F. S. Regs., Part II. and the Staff Manual respectively. Title Pages will be prepared in manuscript.

Place	Date	Hour	Summary of Events and Information	Remarks and references to Appendices
ACHIET-LE-PETIT	11.7.17		Physical Training, Inspection of gun equipment and spare parts	See
-"-	12.7.17		Physical Training, Squad & Arms Drill, Revolver Instruction, Mechanism.	See
-"-	13.7.17		Parades for Divine Service	See
-"-	14.7.17		Revolver Exercises, Gun Drill, Sight setting and laying. Short Route March	See
-"-	15.7.17		Musketry and Revolver Exercises, Sight setting and laying, Squad & Arms Drill Immediate Action	See
-"-	16.7.17		Musketry and Revolver Exercises, Description of Targets, Compulsory Games & Sports.	See
-"-	17.7.17		Musketry and Revolver Exercises, Elementary Tactical Work. Immediate Action. Short Route March	See
-"-	18.7.17		Bayonet Fighting, Rifle Exercises, Squad Drill, Gun Drill, Immediate Action Brigade Training	See
-"-	19.7.17		Rifle Exercises, Gun Drill, Mechanism, Brigade Training	See
-"-	20.7.17		Parades for Divine Service	See
-"-	21.7.17		Squad Drill, Gas Drill, Trench Drill, Rapid Construction of emplacements	See
-"-	22.7.17		Musketry, Revolver Exercises, Gas Drill, Drill with Pack Transport, Short Route March	See

Army Form C. 2118

WAR DIARY
or
INTELLIGENCE SUMMARY
(Erase heading not required.)

127 Machine Gun Company

Sheet 6

Place	Date	Hour	Summary of Events and Information	Remarks and references to Appendices
ACHIET-LE-PETIT.	23.7.17		Packing and unpacking Limbers, Gas Drill, Gun Drill, Company Sports	/tea
— " —	24.7.17		Squad Drill, Gas Drill, Drill with Limbers, Elementary Tactical Exercises, Short Route March.	/tea
— " —	25.7.17		Musketry, Revolver Exercises, Gas Drill, Elementary Tactical Exercises, Immediate Action, Elementary Tactical Exercises with Pack Transport	/tea
— " —	26.7.17		Packing and unpacking Limbers, Gas Drill, Drill with Limbers and Pack Transport, Elementary Tactical Exercises, Brigade Sports.	/tea
— " —	27.7.17		Parades for Divine Services. Brigade Sports.	/tea
— " —	28.7.17		Musketry, Gas Drill, Rapid loading of Pack Animals, Gun Drill, Elementary Tactics with Pack animals and Limbers	/tea
— " —	29.7.17		Drill with Pack Transport, Consolidation of Shell Holes, Rifle Exercises and Company Drill	/tea
— " —	30.7.17		Musketry, Revolver Exercises, Gas Drill, Mechanism, Gun Drill, Packing Limbers, Compulsory Sports.	/tea
— " —	31.7.17		Brigade Training	/tea

APPENDIX No I :- Re-numbering of Guns in new & old Front Lines

F. Aldous Major
Cmdg. 127th Coy. M.G. Corps

Volume VIII   Confidential

War Diary

of

127 Machine Gun Company

Period :- 1st. August 1917 to 31st. August 1917.

Army Form C. 2118.

WAR DIARY
or
INTELLIGENCE SUMMARY
(Erase heading not required.)

127th Machine Gun Company
Sheet No. 1.

Instructions regarding War Diaries and Intelligence Summaries are contained in F.S. Regs., Part II. and the Staff Manual respectively. Title Pages will be prepared in manuscript.

Place	Date	Hour	Summary of Events and Information	Remarks and references to Appendices
			Reference Maps :- 1/40,000 FRANCE. Sheets. 57.C. 57.D. FRANCE & BELGIUM. Sheets. 27. 28.	
ACHIET-LE-PETIT.	1.8.17		Musketry; Squad drill; Elementary Tactical Exercises; Description of Targets.	
"	2.8.17		Rifle Exercises; Squad drill; Practice in M.G. Signals; Games and Sports.	
"	3.8.17		Parades for Divine Services	
"	4.8.17		Musketry; Revolver Exercises; Selection of Positions for Defence; Immediate Action	
"			Overhead Fire.	
"	5.8.17		Rifle Exercises; Squad drill; Selection of Positions for Attack; Immediate Action	
"	6.8.17		Immediate Action; Gas Drill; Elementary Tactical Exercises; Compulsory Games and Sports	
"	7.8.17		Musketry; Revolver Exercises; Immediate Action; Drill with pack animals;	
"			Mechanism; Laying guns for Indirect Fire	
"	8.8.17		Immediate Action; Gas Drill; Tactical scheme with limbers and pack transport;	
"			Games & Sports.	
"	9.8.17		Brigade Training	
"	10.8.17		Parades for Divine Services	
"	11.8.17		Rifle Exercises; Squad drill; Tactical Scheme with Limbers & pack transport.	
"			Consolidation	

WAR DIARY or INTELLIGENCE SUMMARY

Army Form C. 2118.

127th MACHINE GUN COY

Sheet 2.

Place	Date	Hour	Summary of Events and Information	Remarks and references to Appendices
ACHIET-LE-PETIT	12.8.17		Squad drill; Gas drill; Immediate Action; Gun Drill; Barrage Drill.	
"	13.8.17		Musketry, Revolver Exercises; Gas drill; M.G. Signals; Drill from Limbers and Packs. Compulsory Sports	
"	14.8.17		Overhauling Belt Ammunition; Guns and Equipment; Gun Drill; Immediate Action. Belt Filling	
"	15.8.17		Musketry; Gas drill; Elementary Tactical Exercises; Direct Overhead Fire; Reconnaissance of ground for selection of gun positions.	
"	16.8.17		Rifle Exercises; Squad drill; Route March; Games and Sports.	
"	17.8.17		Parades for Divine Services.	
"	18.8.17		Packing and unpacking Limbers; Gas drill; Elementary Tactical Exercises with gas masks; Rifle Exercises; Company drill.	
"	19.8.17		Brigade Training	
"	20.8.17		Squad drill; Overhauling guns and equipment; Immediate Action; Compulsory Sports	
"	21.8.17		At 8.30 A.M. the Company proceeded by march route to AVELUY, and arrived at camping ground at 1 P.M.	

Marching Out :-

OFFICERS.	O.R.	ANIMALS	VEHICLES		BICYCLES
			2 WH	2 WH	
8	178	54	13	2	2

Distance :- 17 KILOS.   Casualties :- 2. O.R.

Army Form C. 2118

127 Machine Gun Coy
Sheet 3

WAR DIARY
or
INTELLIGENCE SUMMARY
(Erase heading not required.)

Place	Date	Hour	Summary of Events and Information	Remarks and references to Appendices
AVELUY	22.8.17		At 10.20 p.m. the Company entrained for HOPOUTRE, detrained at 11 p.m. and marched to camping ground (L.15. B.91.) arriving 12.20 a.m. (23rd inst) Entraining :- OFFICERS 9. O.R. 183 ANIMALS 54. VEHICLES 4 WH — 2WH 13 BICYCLES 3	/a
HOPOUTRE	23.8.17		Cleaning up camp and overhauling equipment and gun stores.	/a
— " —	24.8.17		Squad drill; Immediate Action; Mechanism; Gun drill; Gas Drill; Barrage drill; Visual training	/a
— " —	25.8.17		Semaphore; Elementary Tactical Exercises in gas masks; Company drill; Rifle Exercises; Revolver Instruction	/a
— " —	26.8.17		Parades for Divine Services.	/a
— " —	27.8.17		Company Drill; Immediate Action; Lecture "Machine Guns in attack"; Fire Control; Visual Training; Judging Distance	/a
— " —	28.8.17		Company Drill; Lecture "Co-operation with Infantry and Defence in depth"; Barrage Drill.	/a
— " —	29.8.17		Gun Drill, P.T. and Bayonet Exercises; Immediate Action; Indication and recognition of Targets.	/a
— " —	30.8.17		Company Drill; Gas Drill; Lecture "Initiative"; Games and Sports:	/a
— " —	31.8.17		At 7 a.m. the Company proceeded by march route to G.18a.26 (Sheet 28) and arrived at camp at 10.20 a.m. Distance OFFICERS 10 O.R. 186 ANIMALS 53 VEHICLES 4 WH — 2WH 13 BICYCLES 4. Marching Out :- Casualties: NIL	/a

JG Allens Major
Cmdg. 127th. Coy. M.G. Corps

Confidential
Volume IX

Vol 8

War Diary

of

127th Machine Gun Company

PERIOD:— 1st September 1917 to 30th September 1917

Army Form C. 2118.

127th MACHINE GUN COMPANY.

Sheet 1

WAR DIARY
or
INTELLIGENCE SUMMARY.
(Erase heading not required.)

Place	Date	Hour	Summary of Events and Information	Remarks and references to Appendices
			REFERENCE MAPS:- 1/40,000. FRANCE & BELGIUM Sheets 27 & 28.	
			" 1/20,000 BELGIUM. Sheet. 12	
			" 1/20,000 BELGIUM. Sheet. 12 S.E.	
BRANDHOEK	1.9.17		Overhauling ammunition. Bayonet exercises. Lecture "Barrages"	AGG
-"-	2.9.17		Parades for Divine Services	AGG
-"-	3.9.17		Overhauling equipment and ammunition, Tactical Exercises, Games and Sports.	AGG
-"-	4.9.17		Squad drill, Lecture "Anti-Aircraft Fire" Bayonet fighting. Barrage Drill	AGG
-"-	4/5.9.17		Nos. 2 and 4 Sections moved up and dug indirect fire positions for 8 guns	AGG
			to barrage line D20.a.92. to D14.C.33. in support of attack of 125th INFTY BRIGADE	AGG
-"-	5.9.17		No's 2 and 4 Sections moved up by light railway and march into POTIJZE	AGG
			MILL COTT, and took up indirect fire positions. No's 2 and 4 Sections	AGG
-"-	6.9.17		Attack by 125th INFY. BRIGADE on BECK, BORRY, and IBERIAN.	
			carried out barrage in accordance with programme	AGG
YPRES	7.9.17		Company, less No's 2 and 4 Sections, moved up by railway to ASYLUM and	
			by march route POTIJZE to MILL COTT. Positions taken over in Front	
			Line, 2 guns at SQUARE FARM, 2 guns on right of G in FREZENBURG.	
			Barrage guns were withdrawn	
-"-	8.9.17		No 3 Section moved up to barrage positions behind GREY RUIN.	AGG
			4 guns, No.4 Section, relieved 8 Barrage guns of 125th Coy.	

Army Form C. 2118.

129th MACHINE GUN COMPANY

Sheet 2.

WAR DIARY
or
INTELLIGENCE SUMMARY.
(Erase heading not required.)

Place	Date	Hour	Summary of Events and Information	Remarks and references to Appendices
YPRES	9.9.17		Reconnaissance was made on right and left for positions for attack.	
"	10/11.9.17		Four gun barrage put down on line D.19.b.68 to D.19.b.95. in support of attack on HILL 35 by Brigade on left. Fire was opened at 9.20 P.M. and onwards through the night. In the evening guns redisposed for attack on 12th as follows:- 3 POMMERN CASTLE, 3 APPLE VILLA, 1 LOW FARM, 2 G in FREZENBURG, 3 on right, 4 reserve. These moves were much delayed by hostile barrage but were completed on the night of 10/11th except one gun which was moved into position on the evening of the 11th. Direct fire was opened on BIT WORK and work at D.26.a.21. in support of attack by 126th INFY. BRIGADE.	Appendix Z
"	12.9.17		Six teams were withdrawn in the evening, leaving:- 1 Gun at POMMERN CASTLE, 1 at APPLE VILLA, 1 at LOW FARM, 2 at "G" in FREZENBURG, 1 in Gun Pits.	Appendix R.
"	13.9.17		Guns from POMMERN CASTLE and APPLE VILLA opened direct fire on BREMEN REDOUBT and position about D.20.A.83. POMMERN gun was delayed by shell fire.	
"	14.9.17		The Company was relieved on the line by the 125th COMPANY, proceeding by railway to BRANDHOEK and by march route to TORONTO CAMP.	

Army Form C. 2118

127 MACHINE GUN COMPANY
Sheet 3

WAR DIARY
or
INTELLIGENCE SUMMARY
(Erase heading not required.)

Place	Date	Hour	Summary of Events and Information	Remarks and references to Appendices
BRANDHOEK	15.9.17		Overhauling guns and ammunition	Yes
-"-	16.9.17		Parades for Divine Services	Yes
-"-	17.9.17		The Company proceeded by march route to BRANDHOEK No 2 Area (G.B.B.11) Sheet 27.	Yes
-"-	18.9.17		Revolver Exercises, Inspection of equipment and kit, Games and Sports.	Yes
-"-	19.9.17		At 11.45 A.M. the Company proceeded by march route to HOPOUTRE (L.15.6.9.) Sheet 27. arriving 2.30 P.M. Strength marching out :- O. 7 O.R. 160 Animals 45 Vehicles 2WH 2 4WH 13 Bicycles 4.	Yes
HOPOUTRE	20.9.17		At 7.20 A.M. the Company proceeded by march route to OUDEZEELE (J.9.A.4.3) arriving 1.15 P.M. Strength marching out :- O. 7 O.R. 160 Animals 95. Vehicles 2WH 2 4WH 13 Bicycles 4. Casualties :- Nil. Distance :- 17 Kilos.	Yes
OUDEZEELE	21.9.17		Revolver Exercises, Gas Drill, overhauling guns & equipment, close order drill and rifle exercises. Transport proceeded by march route to COXYDE (sheet 11.) billetting for the night 21/22nd at WORMHOUDT.	Yes
-"-	22.9.17		The Company proceeded by omnibus to COXYDE. embussing 9.30 A.M. Strength embussing 9. Off. 120. O.R. Debussing 1.30 A.M.	Yes

Army Form C. 2118.

WAR DIARY
or
INTELLIGENCE SUMMARY.
(Erase heading not required.)

127 MACHINE GUN COY.
Sheet 4.

Place	Date	Hour	Summary of Events and Information	Remarks and references to Appendices
COXYDE.	23/9/17		Parades for Divine Services	/see
"	24/9/17		Gas drill. Cleaning & overhauling of guns, equipment and limbers. Orders were received to relieve the 204th Coy. in the line	/see
"	25/9/17		Company, less 1 Section, relieved 204th Coy. less 1 Section. Relief began 7.0 A.M. complete 7.30 A.M. 12 gun positions taken over, 8 in front line system. 1 on coast defence.	/see
"	26/9/17		Reconnaissance of ground with a view to increasing defence in depth.	/see
NIEUPORT-BAINS	27/9/17		Three front line positions evacuated & positions taken up at M.21.C.2.4., M.20.b.9.6., M.21.a.6.2.	/see
"	28/9/17		Reconnaissance of Reserve Line	/see
"	29/9/17		Reconnaissance of positions for counter-attack on any part of front line system	/see
"	30/9/17		Position at M.14.d.10.45 evacuated. Position taken up on Island about M.21.b.30. Final dispositions of guns (Appendix 3). Reconnaissance of support position at M.14.c.67. Reconnaissance of ground in front of our front line to cover ground in front of our front line.	/see

APPENDIX 1. Disposition of guns for attack
APPENDIX 2. Disposition of guns for Defence
APPENDIX 3. Disposition of guns, NIEUPORT-BAINS.

L. Gibbons ... Major
C.dg. 127th. Coy. M.G. Corps

Disposition of Guns for Attack

Appendix 1

Scale 1:10,000
Tracing from the map of
Frezenberg Edition 3

DISPOSITION OF GUNS FOR DEFENCE 12/9

APPENDIX 2

SCALE 1:10,000
TRACING FROM THE M
FREZENBERG

Disposition of Guns for Defence

Appendix 3

R M

18
13

Alternative Position

14

M.G. Position at:-
R 23.b.85.35.

20

21

Scale 1:10,000
Tracing taken from map of
Lombartzyde Edition 5

Army Form C. 2118.

WAR DIARY
or
INTELLIGENCE SUMMARY.
(Erase heading not required.)

127th Machine Gun Coy.

Sheet 1

Place	Date	Hour	Summary of Events and Information	Remarks and references to Appendices
			Reference Maps :- 1/40,000 BELGIUM Sheet 11	
			1/20,000 " Sheet 12 S.W.	
NIEUPORT BAINS	1/2.10.17		M.G's fired during the night on the S.O.S. line M.16.d.00 to M.16.d.55.50 (9000 rounds)	Yes
— " —	3.10.17		No.1. Section relieved No.3 Section at 3.A.M. No.4. Section relieved No.2. Section at 9.P.M. No.2 Section proceeding to Transport lines at COXYDE BAINS to rest.	Yes
			Re-disposition of guns completed	(Appendix I)
— " —	4.10.17		M.G's. searched and traversed roads in area M.17.C. (4000 rounds)	Yes
			Indirect fire carried out on area between DENT TRENCH and DEUCE TRENCH (M.9.d) also on GOLF ROAD at M.10.c.03 (4000 rounds)	
— " —	5/6.10.17	R.12. Y.14.	No.2. Section relieved Section of 126th Company, taking over positions R.11, R.11.A.	Yes
— " —	7/8th.10.17	R.12.	Company was relieved by 3 sections of 123rd Company and one section of 124th Company, less No.1. Section, retired to COXYDE BAINS	Yes
			On relief, No.1. Section proceeded to PRESQUILE and relieved a Section of 219th Company.	
COXYDE	9.10.17		Moved to camp at COXYDE. Revolver Instruction, Overhauling gas equipment, guns, and gun equipment.	Yes
			No.9 Section relieved No.1. Section on PRESQUILE	
— " —	10.10.17		Rifle Exercises, Bayonet fighting, Close order drill, Games and Sports.	Yes

Army Form C. 2118.

WAR DIARY
or
INTELLIGENCE SUMMARY
(Erase heading not required.)

127th Machine Gun Coy.
Sheet 2.

Place	Date	Hour	Summary of Events and Information	Remarks and references to Appendices
COXYDE	11.10.17		Physical Training, Construction of dugouts for protection in case of hostile shelling of back area.	See
"	12.10.17		Physical Training, Close order drill, Construction of dug outs	See
"	13.10.17		Physical Training, Construction of dugouts, Games & Sports. Reconnaissance of PRESQUILE and sites for fresh positions located.	See
"	14.10.17		Parades for Divine Service	See
"	15.10.17		Squad drill, Route March, Revolver Range Practices, Tactical Exercises	See
"	16.10.17		Gun drill, Rifle & Revolver Exercises, Concentration of M.G. Fire, Revolver Range Practices, Section relieved a Section of 126th Company on the line.	See
"	17.10.17		Bayonet fighting, Barrage Drill, Map reading and ground reconnaissance. Tactical Exercises, Self protection, Reconnaissance of new Sector.	See
"	18.10.17		No.4 Section relieved by Section of 125th Company in the line Immediate Action, Placing of M.G's to support an attack. Trench foot drill	See
"	19.10.17		Squad Drill, Physical Training, Placing of M.G's in Defence, Construction of dugouts. No. 2. Section relieved on the line by Section of Motor M.G. Company.	See
"	20.10.17		Immediate Action, Lecture "Barrage Drill". Map reading and ground reconnaissance. Games and Sports.	See

Army Form C. 2118.

127th Machine Gun Coy.

Sheet 3.

WAR DIARY
or
INTELLIGENCE SUMMARY.
(Erase heading not required.)

Place	Date	Hour	Summary of Events and Information	Remarks and references to Appendices
COXYDE	21.10.17		Parades for Divine Services. Construction of concrete emplacement on PRESQUILE commenced	Yes
NIEUPORT	22nd/23rd.10.17.	2.0 A.M. 5.30 A.M.	Company, less No. 2. Section, relieved 125th Company, less 1 Section. Relief began 2.0 A.M. Complete 5.30 A.M.	Yes
" "	24.10.17		S.O.S. Barrage for Positions Y9, Y9A, Y9B, Y10. worked out and laid on LOMBARTZYDE. (M22b)	Yes
" "	25.10.17		Guns at Y5 moved from M.28.d.67 to M.29.c.52.65. Regrouping of guns completed. (Appendix II).	Yes
" "	26.10.17		Indirect fire position sited and constructed at M.28.c.25	Yes
" "	26/27.10.17		8 P.M. to 5 A.M. retaliatory M.G. Indirect Fire was brought to bear on Cross Roads M.17.c.02 (750 rounds)	Yes
" "	27/28.10.17		At 6 P.M. and 5 A.M. retaliatory M.G. Indirect Fire was brought to bear on Cross Roads M.17.c.02 (1250 rounds).	Yes
" "	28/29.10.17		In retaliation for hostile M.G. fire, our M.G.'s fired about 800 rounds during the night on Cross Roads, LOMBARTZYDE.	Yes
" "	29/30.10.17		At intervals during the night, retaliatory M.G. Fire was carried out on M.16.c.30.00 (750 rounds).	Yes

Army Form C. 2118.

127th MACHINE GUN COMPANY.
Sheet 7.

WAR DIARY
or
INTELLIGENCE SUMMARY.
(Erase heading not required.)

Place	Date	Hour	Summary of Events and Information	Remarks and references to Appendices
NIEUPORT.	30th/31.10.17.		During the night retaliatory M.G. fire was carried out on M.16.G. 30.00 (1000 rounds)	See
	31.10.17	5.30 P.M.	At 5.30 P.M. guns from positions Y9A, Y9B, were withdrawn and took over positions Y11B, Y11C, from 11th Motor M.G. Btty. on PRESQU'ILE. A.A. gun at Y9A. moved to Y10.	See
			Appendix I - 127th M.G. Coy. Defence Orders, NIEUPORT BAINS Sector	
			Appendix II - Disposition of machine-guns, LOMBARTZYDE Sector	

Haddons   Major
Cmdg. 127th. Coy. M.G. Corps

SECRET.   COPY: No 13.

127th M.G. Coy. Defence Orders.

Ref. Map.   Sheet 4. } 1/10,000
            Sheet 5.

1. **General Principles**
   A. Every man of a gun team must know the duty of his own gun in case of attack.
   B. It is essential that the machine guns continue fighting although the infantry are driven back, as they may easily stop the attack by their fire alone.
   C. In face of hostile bombardment, guns in concrete emplacements will be kept mounted. Those not in concrete will be dismounted and placed in the dugout; an observer must be left up who will give warning of an infantry attack, when the gun will be at once mounted.

2. **Disposition**
   The guns are disposed in groups as shown on attached sketch. One gun (Y14) of REMNANT detachment is, however, under O.C. No. 1. Section for fire orders. No 2. Section are in reserve at rear headquarters, COXYDE BAINS.

3. **M.G. Defence**
   This consists of:
   (a) Guns defending front line
   (b) Guns in support sweeping front line and ground behind it in case it is captured.
   (c) Guns in the reserve line.
   (d) Coast Defence

4. **Action in case of attack**
   (a) Guns in the front line will open fire on their S.O.S. line. But if the S.O.S. signal is sent up and there are no signs of attack along their S.O.S. line they will not open fire except at night.
   (b) Guns in support will stand by. If the front line is taken they will annihilate any hostile troops that have broken through & will prevent a further advance. They will support counter-attacks by enfilading the front line.

(Appendix I)
To Accompany Defence Orders dated 9.10.17

R. M.
18 — 13 — 15

. C4
P Coy H.Q & Section H.Q.
24 — 19 — 20 — 21

. C3
. R17
. R16
R15
. Y17
. Y18
Y18A
P Y19 Section H.Q.
14
. Y15
Y17A
P Section H.Q. Y13 Y14
Y12
. R12
P Section H.Q.
. R11A
. R11

Confidential
Vol. X

Vol 9

War Diary

of

127th Machine Gun Company.

Period :- 1st October 1917 to 31st October 1917

Volume XI   Confidential

War Diary

of

127th Machine Gun Company

Period :- 1st November 1917 to 30th November 1917.

Army Form C. 2118

127th Machine Gun Company

Sheet 1.

WAR DIARY
or
INTELLIGENCE SUMMARY
(Erase heading not required.)

Instructions regarding War Diaries and Intelligence Summaries are contained in F.S. Regs., Part II. and the Staff Manual respectively. Title Pages will be prepared in manuscript.

Place	Date	Hour	Summary of Events and Information	Remarks and references to Appendices
			Reference Maps:- 1/40,000 Belgium Sheet 11.	
			1/20,000 " " 12. S.W.	
			1/40,000 BETHUNE. (Combined Sheet) 36.S.W. 36ᴬ N.E. 36ᴬ S.E. 36ᴬ N.W.	
			1/100,000 DUNKERQUE. Sheet.1A. HAZEBROUCK. Sheet. 5A.	
NIEUPORT.	31st Oct 1-11-17		During the night retaliatory M.G. Fire was carried out on M.16.d. 86.79 (500 rounds)	74
"	2nd 2-11-17		During the night retaliatory M.G. Fire was carried out on M.16.d. 86.79 (750 rounds)	74
"	2nd and 3rd 3-11-17		In retaliation for hostile M.G. Fire, Indirect fire was carried out on M.16.d.53.47. (2750 rounds)	74
"	3-11-17		Two guns of 11th M.M.G. Btty. were withdrawn from positions Y.11. Y.11A. and occupied positions Y.9. Y.9.a.	74
			Two guns of the Company were withdrawn from Y.11d. Y.11.a. and occupied positions Y.13. (M.21.a.72.10) and Y.14. (M.21.a.75.06) to bring fire to bear on LORRY TRENCH and LORRY WALK. Withdrawal commenced 5.30 p.m. completed 7.30 p.m.	
"	3rd 4-11-17		During the night retaliatory M.G. Fire was carried out on M.16.d. 87.74 (1500 rounds) and on M.16.d. 82.20 (750 rounds).	74
"	4th 5-11-17		During the night retaliatory fire was carried out by our M.G's on M.16.d. 86.79 74. (2250 rounds).	74

Army Form C. 2118

WAR DIARY
or
INTELLIGENCE SUMMARY
(Erase heading not required.)

127th Machine Gun Coy

Sheet 2

Place	Date	Hour	Summary of Events and Information	Remarks and references to Appendices
NIEUPORT.	5th 6/4-11-17		During the night retaliatory M.G. Fire was carried out on M.17.C.0760 and M.16.d.8576 (2150 rounds).	JH.
— " —	6th 6/7-11-17		During the night retaliatory M.G. Fire was carried out on M.17.C.0758 (3225 rounds)	JH.
	7-11-17		Company, less No. 2 Section, was relieved in the line by three Sections of 125th Company. On relief each Section proceeded independently to COXYDE to rest.	JH. JH.
COXYDE	8-11-17		Cleaning and overhauling guns, equipment and spare parts	JH.
— " —	9-11-17		Revolver Exercises, Cleaning and overhauling guns, equipment and spare parts. Revolver Instruction	JH.
— " —	10-11-17		Washing down and cleaning limbers.	JH.
— " —	11-11-17		Parades for Divine Service	JH.
— " —	11th 12.-11.-17.		Two Sections co-operated with Division on our right who executed a raid on TERSTILLE FARM. S.A.A. Expended 8,500 rounds. Casualties:- 1 O.R. wounded.	JH.
— " —	13-11-17		Four guns and teams were attached to 126th Company in the line	JH.
— " —	14-11-17		Revolver Instruction, Barrage Drill, Recreational Training, Immediate Action. Stripping, cleaning, and refilling belts. Party employed in construction of concrete emplacement on PRESQUILE, also four guns in the line, were withdrawn	JH. JH.

Army Form C. 2118.

WAR DIARY
or
INTELLIGENCE SUMMARY.
(Erase heading not required.)

141st Machine Gun Coy
Sheet 3

Place	Date	Hour	Summary of Events and Information	Remarks and references to Appendices
COXYDE	15.11.17		Squad drill, Barrage Drill, Immediate Action, Games (compulsory)	JM
—	16.11.17		Company entrained COXYDE 10 P.M. detrained LEFFRINCKHOUCKE 3.0 A.M. and traversed by march-route to TETEGHEM, arriving 5.30 A.M.	JM
TETEGHEM	17.11.17		Company continued its march, marching out 8.40 A.M. arrived WORMHOUDT 4.15 P.M. Casualties 1 O.R.	JM
WORMHOUDT	18.11.17		Company continued its march, marching out 7.40 A.M. arrived HARDIFORT 10 A.M.	JM
HARDIFORT	19.11.17		Company continued its march marching out 8.50 A.M. arrived STAPLE AREA. 11.15 A.M.	JM
STAPLE AREA	20.11.17		Company continued its march, marching out 6.50 A.M. arrived BERGUETTE 4.15 P.M. Strength marching out from COXYDE :- OFF. 8 O.R. 153 ANIMALS 54 VEHICLES 4 4MM. 13 BM 2. BICYCLES 4. The whole distance covered was approx. 70 miles; number of casualties being 1. O.R. for the whole march.	JM
BERGUETTE	21.11.17		Cleaning and overhauling of equipment.	JM
"	22.11.17		Recruits Instruction, Recreational Training, Barrage Drill, Games and Sports	JM
"	23.11.17		Recruits Instruction, Immediate Action, Barrage Drill	JM
"	24.11.17		Gas helmet drill, Inspection of guns and equipment, Games & Sports	JM
"	25.11.17		Parades for Divine Services	JM

Army Form C. 2118.

WAR DIARY
or
INTELLIGENCE SUMMARY
(Erase heading not required.)

127 Machine Gun Coy
Sheet 4.

Place	Date	Hour	Summary of Events and Information	Remarks and references to Appendices
BERGUETTE CO.I.WE	26-11-17		The Company proceeded by march route to OBLINGHEM, marching out 3.15 p.m. arrived OBLINGHEM.	7x.
— " —	27-11-17		The Company continued its march, marching out 12.30 p.m. arrived GORRE 4.30 p.m. Casualties 1 M.T.	7x.
GORRE.	28-11-17		The Company relieved the 7th M.G. Coy. in the GIVENCHY Sector, 4 guns in left Sector, 5 guns in right Sector, 7 guns in Barrage positions. Relief commenced 4.0 a.m., completed 6.30 a.m.	(Appendix I) 7x.
GIVENCHY SECTOR	29-11-17	7.0 p.m. - 7.30 p.m.	M.G. Fire carried out against Cross Roads in VIOLAINES, A.5.d. 75.95, and also on road from A.10.d. 87. - R.10.d. 86. S.A.A. Expended = 800 rounds.	7x.
— " —	30-11-17 / 1.12.17		During the night M.G. fire was carried out against area R.10.a. 8020 - R.10.d. 9065, one gun firing 800 rounds, the other 1500 rounds; also two M.Gs fired on area A.10.d. 85. - A.16.d. 1570., each gun firing 1500 rounds.	7x.

APPENDIX I   Disposition of M.Gs in GIVENCHY SECTOR.

Bevys Capt.
CAPT.
Cmdg. 127 Machine Gun Coy.

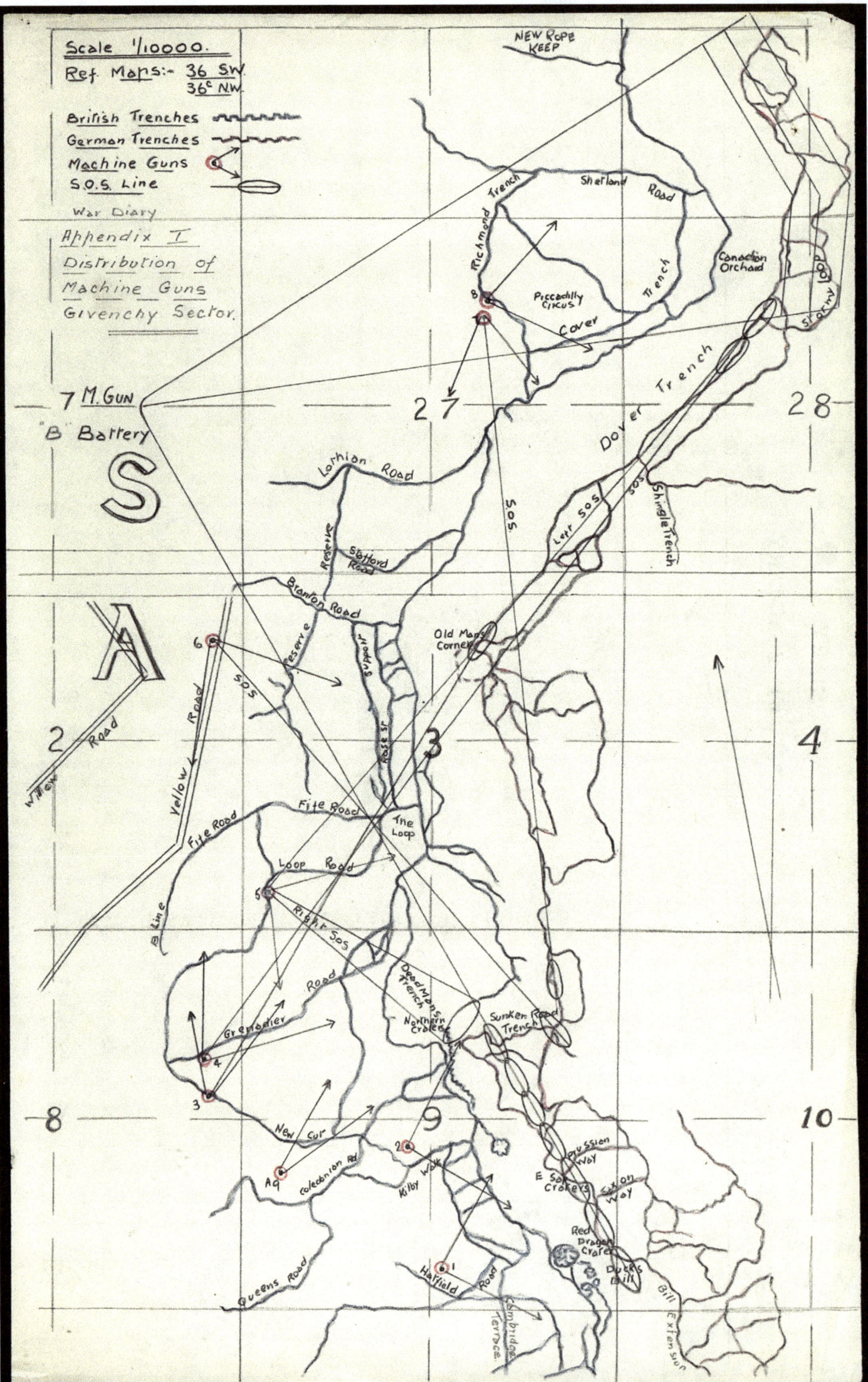

Volume XII   *Confidential*

War Diary
of
127 Machine Gun Company

Period :- 1st. December to 31st. December 1917

Volume XII
Army Form C. 2118.

127th Machine Gun Coy

WAR DIARY
or
INTELLIGENCE SUMMARY.
(Erase heading not required.)

Place	Date	Hour	Summary of Events and Information	Remarks and references to Appendices
Givenchy Sector			Reference Maps:- 36 S.W. 36 C. N.W.	
	1/12/17		During the night two of our MGs fired on Cross Roads Violaines. A5d 65.95. SAA expended 3000 rounds. One gun fired on Brick Fields. A5a 1060. SAA. expended 1500 rounds.	J.W.B.
	2/3-12-17		During the night 2500 rounds were fired on road A10a 8666 - A10d 7972 and 1250 rounds on area round A10d 8466.	J.W.B.
	3/12/17		During the day 2500 rounds were fired on CROSS ROADS A6a 4237 and ROAD JUNCTION, VIOLAINES, A5d 6595.	J.W.B.
	4/12/17		During the night (3/4") 7000 rounds were fired on REDOUBT ALLEY SOUTH A2a 6075 - A4 6070. Also 2 guns and road A3d 95 - A2a 64. During the day 2500 rounds were fired on Cross Roads A11c 9.535.	J.W.B.
	5/12/17		During the night 4/5" 6050 rounds were fired on road A10a 8565 - A10d 7075 and Cross Roads VIOLAINES. A5d 6595. During the day 1250 rounds were fired on Cross Roads A62 4237.	J.W.B.
	6/12/17		During the night (5/6") 10,000 rounds were fired on road A10d 94 to A16d17 and Junction A10c 93 to A10d 86. During the day 2500 rounds were fired on Trenches and road S29a 3755 - S29 6.18.15. Nos 1 and a sections relieved No2 and 3 Sections. Rely commenced 8 a.m. Completed 11.30 a.m.	J.W.B.
	7/12/17		During the night (6/7") 6500 rounds were fired on road S29 6 1519 - A5b 7560 and road A5a 3950 - A5.6 5785. During the day 2500 rounds were fired on CROSS ROADS and 13m H.A. S29d 3555.	J.W.B.
	8/12/17		During the night (7/8") 4500 rounds were fired on Road Junction CANTELEUX A10d 9565. Junct S25c 3330 to A4a 6070 and T Roads Rue du Marais S29a 6656. During the day 1050 rounds were fired on BRICKFIELDS A5a 1060.	J.W.B.

Page 2.

Army Form C. 2118.

WAR DIARY
or
INTELLIGENCE SUMMARY.
(Erase heading not required.)

127th Machine Gun Coy.
Volume XII Contd.

Instructions regarding War Diaries and Intelligence Summaries are contained in F. S. Regs., Part II. and the Staff Manual respectively. Title pages will be prepared in manuscript.

Place	Date	Hour	Summary of Events and Information	Remarks and references to Appendices
Givenchy Sector.	9.12.17		During the night (8/9) 2000 rounds were fired on Rue du Marais S28a 8020 – S29a 4260 and BRICKFIELDS A5a 35.	JWB
	10.12.17		During the night (9/10th) 1800 rounds were fired on Roads and Trenches Aad 1035 & A5a 0026.	JWB
	11.12.17		During the day 600 rounds were fired onto T Roads, Rue du Marais S29a 6856 A4b 6070 During the night (10/11) 2000 rounds were fired on. REDOUBT ALLEY SOUTH A42 6075 –	JWB
	12.12.17		During the night (11/12) 1900 rounds were fired on area A9d 55 and A10a 79. During the day 900 rounds were fired on X Roads A10a 7080.	JWB
	12/13/17		During the night (12/13th) 2400 rounds were fired on Rue du Marais S28a 8520 – S29a 2250 and T. Roads S29a 6856; also 2000 rounds on A10c 8090 – A16d 0050 Nos 2 and 3 Sections relieved Nos 1 and 4 Section. Relief commenced 9 a.m. Completed 12.3 a.m. During the day 600 rounds were fired on Redoubt Alley South H42 6075 – A4 b 6070.	JWB
	14.12.17		During the night (13/14th) 1100 rounds were fired on line A10a 7090 – A16a 9055 also 1150 rounds on Road from A10a 9565 – A10d 7575.	JWB
	15.12.17		During the night 3300 rounds were fired on S29a 4060. Major F.C. ALDOUS attached OMGO to 61st Division, CAPTAIN G.J. NORRIS (from 113/MGC) assumed command of the Company.	JWB
	16.12.17		During the night 2600 rounds were fired on East side of drain A5c06 and Road A4c 9526 – A10a 9585.	JWB
	17.12.17		During the night 1800 rounds were fired on Cross Roads GH 44 to S4 IPOCH and Road A10a 8468 – A10d 8280. During the day 600 rounds were fired on B.H.Q S29 a 2577 and Brickfields A5a 1060. Nos 1 and 4 Sections relieved Nos 2 and 3 Section. Relief commenced 9 a.m. Completed 2.0 a.m.	JWB

Volume XI Cont'd
Army Form C. 2118.
Page 3.

127th Machine Gun Coy.

WAR DIARY
or
INTELLIGENCE SUMMARY.
(Erase heading not required.)

Place	Date	Hour	Summary of Events and Information	Remarks and references to Appendices
Givenchy Sector	18.12.17		During the night 2400 rounds were fired on Brickfields A5a 1060. During the day 500 rounds were fired on Roads A3t.9544 to A4c.3545 and S28.c.3832 - S29a.3857	JWB
	19.12.17		During the night 1600 rounds were fired on Rue du Marias S28a 8318 - S29a 2250 and area within 500x of A10a 8560.	JWB
	20.12.17		During the night 3000 rounds were fired on Bn. H.Q. S29a 2577. During the day 600 rounds were fired on Cross Roads A10a 7080.	JWB
	21.12.17		During the night 1650 rounds were fired on A+L 2000 - A11a 4065. During the day 500 rounds were fired on A10a 0565 - A10 0515.	JWB
	22.12.17		During the night 1950 rounds were fired on A5a 1060 and Road S28a 8318 - S29a 2509	JWB
	23.12.17		During the night 3400 rounds were fired on REDOUBT ALLEY SOUTH A+c 6075 - A+c 5070 and BRICKFIELDS A5a 1060. The Company was relieved in the line by the 125th M.G. Coy.(+ two guns and a enfilade section remaining in the line for duty as Battery for barrage purposes under command of G.O.C. 125th Brigade. Relief commenced 4 A.M. Completed 6 A.M. on relief each section marched independently to GORRE when breakfast was served and the men cleaned themselves, after which company proceeded by march route to BÉTHUNE (MONTMORENCY BARRACKS) marching and. arriving BÉTHUNE 11.30 a.m. Casualties Nil.	JWB
BÉTHUNE.	24.12.17		Cleaning up of guns and equipment. Inspection by C.O. Chaines.	JWB
	25.12.17		Christmas Day. Parades for Divine Service.	JWB

Army Form C. 2118.

WAR DIARY
or
INTELLIGENCE SUMMARY.
(Erase heading not required.)

127th Machine Gun Company

Volume VII   Page 4

Place	Date	Hour	Summary of Events and Information	Remarks and references to Appendices
BÉTHUNE	26·12·17		Gun Drill. Immediate Action. Squad Drill. Physical Training. Gas Drill and Barrage Drill. The Composite Section, attached to the 125th Company, M.G.C. for Barrage work, was relieved by another Composite Section. During the afternoon Interunion football matches were played.	J W G
	27·12·17		Gun Drill, Immediate Action, Close Order Drill, Gas Drill and Barrage Drill. A lecture was given by the C.O. on "Aeroplane Sights." A Reconnaissance was carried out by an officer and 2 O.Rs. of the 138th Brigade Reserve Line. During the afternoon the Company moved from BÉTHUNE to Billets in ESSARS. The Company marched out at 1.30 pm and arrived at 2.45 pm. Casualties:- Nil.	J W G
ESSARS.	28·12·17		Section Officers Inspection and Bathing. Tennis and Sports. A party of 9 O.Rs. were attached to the 170th Tunnelling Company, for the purpose of constructing M.G. Emplacements. A reconnaissance was made by an officer and 2 O.Rs of the Grenay – Noyelles line.	J W G
	29·12·17		Immediate Action. Range practice and overhauling of guns. Games and Sports. The Composite Section attached to the 125th M.G. Coy. was relieved by another Composite Section. A reconnaissance was made of the Corps Reserve line, by an officer and 2 O.Rs.	J W G
	30·12·17		The Company attended a ceremonial parade for the presentation of medals by the G.O.C. Division at W17 Central.	J W G
	31·12·17		Barrage Drill. During the morning the Company paraded for Bathing during the afternoon. Divisional Gas School for a lecture. Gas Transport attended the afternoon. All Gas Helmets were tested. The afternoon was spent in Range Practice.	J W G

J. W. Dennett Lieut.
Capt.
Cmdg. 127th. Coy. M. G. Corps

VOLUME I
4 Pages.   Confidential

War Diary

of

127th. Machine Gun Company

Period:— 1st. January 1918 to 31st. January 1918

Confidential
Army Form C. 2118
Volume I
Page I

WAR DIARY
or
INTELLIGENCE SUMMARY
(Erase heading not required.)

127 Machine Gun Company

Instructions regarding War Diaries and Intelligence Summaries are contained in F.S. Regs., Part II. and the Staff Manual respectively. Title Pages will be prepared in manuscript.

Place	Date	Hour	Summary of Events and Information	Remarks and references to Appendices
ESSARS	1.1.18		Reference Maps:- 36ᶜ N.W.1 / 36 S.W.3. Immediate Action. Lecture on writing messages and map signs by Section Officers. Rough Ground Drill. Games and Sports. During the morning the Transports Section and a few details attended the Divisional Gas School for a lecture and gas test. No.1 Section relieved the Composite Section, attached to the 126th M.G. Coy for Barrage work, at Cailloux Post South.	GH
	2.1.18		Mechanism. Close Order drill. Barrage Drill and Rough Ground Drill. Games and Sports. A reconnaissance was made of the (La Bassée) Right Sector by the Commanding Officer.	GH
	3.1.18		Close Order Drill. Barrage Drill. Overhauling gun equipment and packing limbers. A reconnaissance was made of the (La Bassée) Right Sector, prior to taking over the line from the 126th M.G. Coy.	GH
	3rd/4th. 1.1.18		During the night of the 3rd/4th the Company relieved the 126th M.G. Coy in the line. No.2 Section plus one team of No.3 Section and one team of No.4 Section relieved "A" Group, with Section H.Q. at A14.c.2025. One Section from "A" Group 126th M.G. Coy relieved No.1 Section on Cailloux Post South. No.4 Section less one team relieved "B" Group, with Section H.Q. at No.9 Buckshot. No.3 Section less two m. team relieved "C" Group with Section H.Q. at A15.a.4560. No.1 Section relieved "D" Group with Section H.Q. at A21.c.0030. The relief was commenced at 3pm on the 3rd and completed by 10.35 am on the 4th. Company H.Q. being established at Le Preol. F.15.b.75. Casualties:- Nil. Appendix I	GH
Givenchy Right Sector	4.1.18			
	5.1.18		During the night MG harassing fire was carried out on Targets A29.a.9085 and A17.c.2525. 5.H.A. expended 1500 rounds. Positions were cleaned up and improved. 3000 rounds were fired during the night on Targets A17.a.1060 and A29.c.5070. Emplacements were improved and dug outs strengthened.	GH

Confidential
Army Form C. 2118
Volume 7
127 Machine Gun Company
Page 2

WAR DIARY
or
INTELLIGENCE SUMMARY

(Erase heading not required.)

Place	Date	Hour	Summary of Events and Information	Remarks and references to Appendices
Givenchy Right Sector	6th/7th.1.18		During the night 2250 rounds were fired on A22 b 2060 and A28 b 6080. Work was continued on positions and dugouts.	GPh
	7/8.1.18		During the night 2250 rounds were fired on Targets A17c 2525 and A29 a 2530.	GPh
	8/9.1.18		During the night 1500 rounds were fired on Target A29a 9085 and A17c 2525.	GPh
	9/10.1.18		Work was continued on all emplacements and dugouts were strengthened.	GPh
	10/11.1.18		During the night 1500 rounds were fired on Railway Crossing A22 b 85.	GPh
	11th/12.1.18		During the night 1500 rounds were fired on Road Junction A29 b 08.	GPh
	13.1.18		A reconnaissance was made, by the Commanding Officer, of Machine Gun positions in the VILLAGE LINE. Work was continued on all occupied positions.	GPh
	14/15.1.18		A reconnaissance of The Port Fixe locality was carried out by the Brigade Major 127th Brigade, and the Commanding Officer, to decide upon strong points of resistance. During the night 1500 rounds were fired on Cross Roads A23a 4.6.	GPh
	15/16.1.18		A further reconnaissance was carried out by The Brigadier General, 127th Brigade, and the Commanding Officer, of strong points in The Village Defence Line. During the night 1500 rounds were fired on LONE FARM, A29 a 3.0.	GPh
	16.1.18		1500 rounds rapid, were fired from emplacement PF5 in presence of 1st Army Representative, for the purpose of ascertaining the effect of the gases on the gun team in an enclosed position. Owing to wind the steam and gases were dispersed and no ill effects were felt by those in the emplacement.	GPh
	17.1.18		During the night 1500 rounds were fired on A17 b. 25.15 (TRENCH JUNCTION)	GPh
	18.1.18		During the night 750 rounds were fired on to Target A10d. 95.65.	GPh
	19.1.18		During the night 1500 rounds were fired on "SPOTTED DOG", LA BASSEE ROAD.	GPh

Army Form C. 2118.
Volume I
Page 3

WAR DIARY
or
INTELLIGENCE SUMMARY.
(Erase heading not required.)

127th Machine Gun Company

Instructions regarding War Diaries and Intelligence Summaries are contained in F.S. Regs., Part II. and the Staff Manual respectively. Title pages will be prepared in manuscript.

Place	Date	Hour	Summary of Events and Information	Remarks and references to Appendices
GIVENCHY RIGHT SECTOR	20/1/18		During the night 1600 rounds were fired on ROAD & TRENCH JUNCTION (A23a. 2.4)	G/R
"	21-1-18		During the night M.Gs. fired 1500 rounds on TOW PATH (A17c 30.45)	G/R
"	22-1-18		20 O.R. from 268 M.G. Coy were attached to teams in the line for instruction in Trench Duties	G/R
"	23-1-18		During the night 1500 rounds were fired on ROAD (A23c 28.25)	G/R
"	24-1-18		The party of 20 O.R. from 268 M.G. Coy, attached to teams in the line for instruction was relieved by a similar party	G/R
"			During the night 1500 rounds were fired on RAILWAY CROSSING (A22b 85.50)	G/R
"	25-1-18		During the night 1500 rounds were fired on TOW PATH (A17c 30 45)	G/R
"	26-1-18		The party of 20 O.R. from 268 M.G. Coy was relieved by a similar party	G/R
"			During the night 1500 rounds were fired on MINNIE ROAD	G/R
"	27-1-18		During the night 1500 rounds were fired on to LONE FARM (A29a)	G/R
"	28-1-18		The 20 O.R. attached from 268 M.G. Coy. proceeded to rejoin their unit	G/R
"			During the night 1500 rounds were fired on ROAD (A17b)	G/R
"			At 6 P.M. 1500 rounds rapid, were fired from emplacement PF5 in the presence of 1st Army Representative. There was no wind and no ill effects were felt by those in the emplacement.	
"	29-1-18		A reconnaissance was made, of the (LA BASSEE) Right Sector by Officers of the 125th M.G. Coy. prior to taking over the line.	G/R

Army Form C. 2118.
Volume I

WAR DIARY
or
INTELLIGENCE SUMMARY.
127th Machine Gun Company Page 4
(Erase heading not required.)

Instructions regarding War Diaries and Intelligence Summaries are contained in F. S. Regs., Part II. and the Staff Manual respectively. Title pages will be prepared in manuscript.

Place	Date	Hour	Summary of Events and Information	Remarks and references to Appendices
GIVENCHY RIGHT SECTOR	30/1/18		The Company was relieved in the line by the 125th. M.G. Coy. Relief commenced 10 A.M. completed by 11 P.M. On relief sections marched independently to billets at ESSARS. Casualties - NIL	GMc.
ESSARS	31/1/18		Cleaning and checking of all gun stores and equipment. Bathing.	GMc.
			Appendices I Disposition of M.Gs. in GIVENCHY RIGHT SECTOR	

G. McNeil Capt.
Comdg. 127th. Coy. M. G. Corps

War Diary
Appendix I
Shewing disposition of M.G.s

PART OF SHEET 36° N.W.1.

Scale :- 1:10000

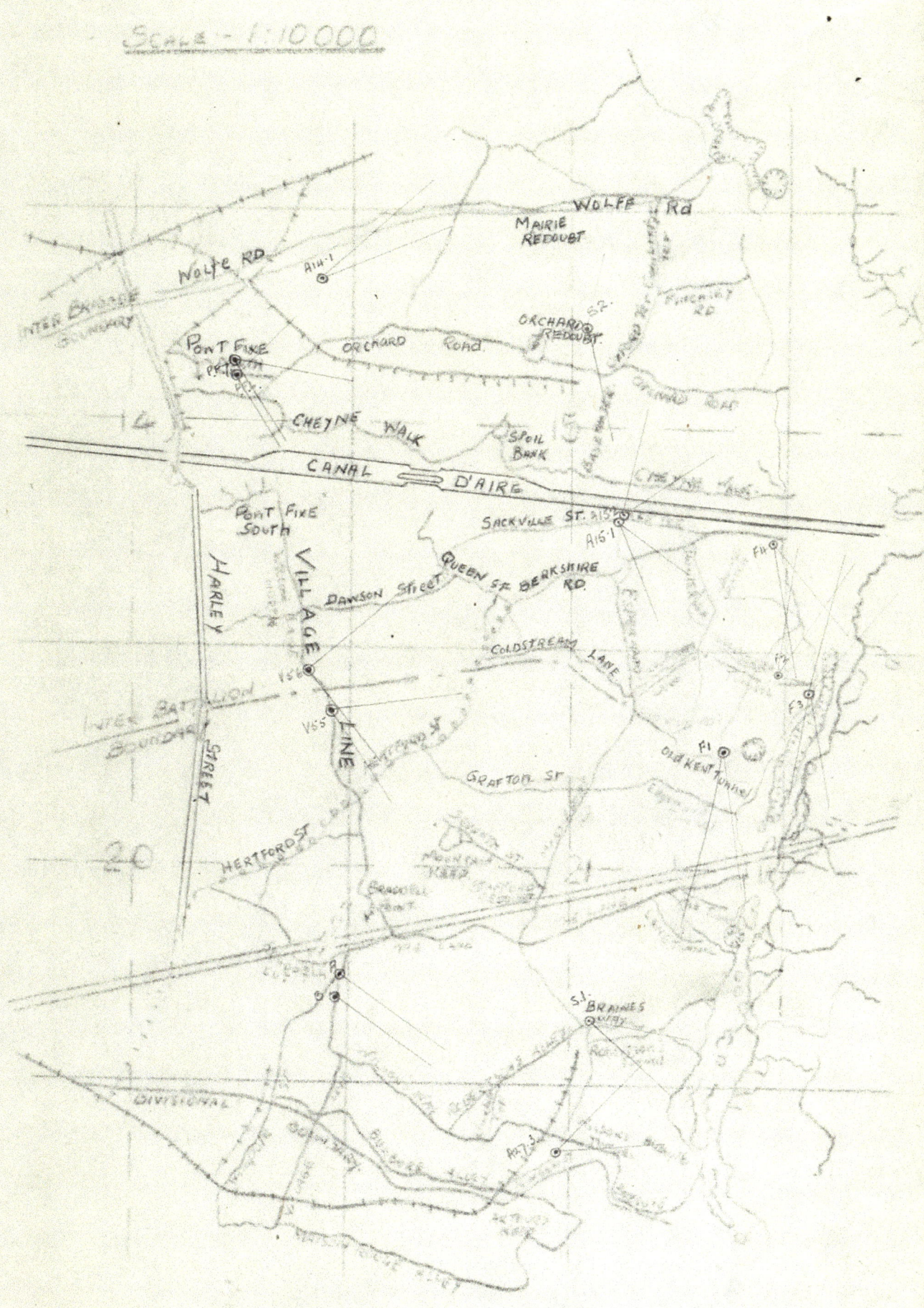

127th M.G.Coy

Volume II

<u>Confidential</u>

<u>War Diary</u>

of

<u>127 Machine Gun Company</u>

<u>Period:- 1st. February 1918 to 28th. February 1918.</u>

Army Form C. 2118.
VOLUME II
SHEET 1.

WAR DIARY
or
INTELLIGENCE SUMMARY.

127 Machine Gun Company

(Erase heading not required.)

Instructions regarding War Diaries and Intelligence Summaries are contained in F. S. Regs., Part II. and the Staff Manual respectively. Title pages will be prepared in manuscript.

Place	Date	Hour	Summary of Events and Information	Remarks and references to Appendices
			REF: MAPS:- BETHUNE (combined sheet) SHEET 36 B.	
ESSARS	1-2-18		Inspection of Revolvers, Guns & Stores on Mobilisation Table. Bathing	
"	2-2-18		Revolver Practice, Lecture on "War Savings" Bathing	
"	3-2-18		Parade for Divine Service	
"	4-2-18		Revolver & N.G. Range Practice	
"	5-2-18		Care and Cleaning, Revolver Instruction, Lecture by Section Officers	
"	6-2-18		Care and Cleaning, Revolver Instruction, Lecture by Section Officers, Games & Sports	
"	7-2-18		Revolver Instruction & Range Practice, Map Reading	
"	8-2-18		Gas Lecture & Instruction under Divisional Gas Officer, Revolver Instruction & Range Practice, Games & Sports	
"	9-2-18		Gas Lecture & Instruction under Divisional Gas Officer, Revolver Range, Football match	
"	10-2-18		Parade for Divine Service	
"	11-2-18		Overhauling guns & equipment, issue of small kit, packing limbers	
"	12-2-18		The Company proceeded by march route to billets at LABEUVRIERE, marching out 8.15 A.M. arrived 10.30 A.M. Distance:- 9 KMS. Casualties = NIL. The afternoon was spent in cleaning billets.	
LA BEUVRIERE	13-2-18		Close Order Drill by Sections, I.A. and Causes of Stoppages, Lecture by Section Officers. Sports	

WAR DIARY
or
INTELLIGENCE SUMMARY.

127 Machine Gun Company

Army Form C. 2118.
VOLUME II
SHEET 2

Place	Date	Hour	Summary of Events and Information	Remarks and references to Appendices
LABEUVRIERE	14-2-18		Close Order Drill, Elementary Gun Drill, Lecture on Sanitation, Bathing.	GH
"	15-2-18		Short Route March, Gun Drill, Sports	GH
"	16-2-18		Inspection by Lt Col W.K. Tullie M.C. D.M.G.O. Indication & Recognition of targets. Recreational Training	GH
"	17-2-18		Parade for Divine Service	GH
"	18-2-18		Company Parade – Steady Drill & Saluting, P.T., Barrage Drill	GH
"	19-2-18		P.T. Barrage Drill, Lecture.	GH
"	20-2-18		Company Parade – Steady Drill & Saluting, Barrage Drill. Demonstration by each Section Officer (1) Laying on gun by compass (2) Laying out parallel lines by compass	GH
"	21-2-18		Demonstration of Guard Mounting, Barrage Drill. Games & Sports	GH
"	22-2-18		P.T. Barrage Drill & Packsaddling Drill. Lecture by M.O. on "Sanitation."	GH
"	23-2-18		Bathing, Gas Drill, Sports	GH
"	24-2-18		Parade for Divine Service	GH
"	25-2-18		Company Parade – Steady Drill, Handling of Arms, Saluting, Gas Drill, P.T. 2 Officers of this Company and Officers of the 127th Inf. Brigade made a general reconnaissance of the defences of the PHILOSOPHE – NOYELLES – NOEUX-LES-MINES localities.	GH

WAR DIARY
or
INTELLIGENCE SUMMARY.
(Erase heading not required.)

Army Form C. 2118

VOLUME II
SHEET 3

127 Machine Gun Company

Place	Date	Hour	Summary of Events and Information	Remarks and references to Appendices
LABEUVRIERE	26-2-18		A detailed reconnaissance was made, by all ranks of the Company, of the defences of PHILOSOPHE – NOYELLES – NOEUX-LES-MINES localities and positions which would be occupied in case of a hostile attack.	Offr.
—	27-2-18		Training	Offr.
—	28-2-18		Training	Offr.

C. Howard Capt.
Cmdg. 127th. Coy. M. G. Corps

www.ingramcontent.com/pod-product-compliance
Lightning Source LLC
Chambersburg PA
CBHW081557160426
43191CB00011B/1958